ALEXIS CARREL

# Alexis Carrel

## VISIONARY SURGEON

By

### W. STERLING EDWARDS, M.D.

*Professor and Chairman Department of Surgery*

*University of New Mexico School of Medicine*

*Albuquerque, New Mexico*

*and*

### PETER D. EDWARDS

*With a Foreword by*
**Charles A. Lindbergh**

**CHARLES C THOMAS · PUBLISHER**

*Springfield · Illinois · U. S. A.*

*Published and Distributed Throughout the World by*

CHARLES C THOMAS · PUBLISHER

Bannerstone House

301–327 East Lawrence Avenue, Springfield, Illinois, U.S.A.

*With THOMAS BOOKS careful attention is given to all details of manufacturing
and design. It is the Publisher's desire to present books that are satisfactory as to
their physical qualities and artistic possibilities and appropriate for their particular
use. THOMAS BOOKS will be true to those laws of quality that assure a good
name and good will.*

**Library of Congress Cataloging in Publication Data**

Edwards, William Sterling, 1920–
    Alexis Carrel:  visionary surgeon.

    1. Carrel, Alexis, 1873–1944.  2. Heart—Surgery.
3. Blood-vessels—Surgery.  I. Edwards, Peter D., joint
author. [DNLM:  1. History of medicine—Biology.
WZ100 C3133 E 1974]
R507.C34E36          617′.41′0924 [B]          74–717
ISBN 0–398–03130–4

*Printed in the United States of America*

K-8

# ALEXIS CARREL

SCIENTIST AND MYSTIC, now in the van of civilized progress, now retiring from it, Doctor Alexis Carrel was one of the most extraordinary and controversial figures of his generation. Bearing a fame that spread around the planet, he was decorated and damned, often by the same people.

Carrel's Nobel Prize in surgery contrasted with charges of charlatanism levied against him when he wrote articles for popular magazines, discussed extrasensory perception, and advanced radical ideas for remaking mankind. A deeply patriotic Frenchman, he was accused of collaboration during the German occupation of World War II. Having achieved the heights of acclaim, he died in despair. Recently, medical scientists evaluating his work in the light of modern developments have said that he was fifty to a hundred years ahead of his time.

Carrel devoted much of his professional life to medical research in New York City's ultra civilization. By his desire, his body lies buried on the wild, rocky, and tide-isolated island of Saint Gildas off the Breton coast of his native country. New York and Saint Gildas typically span his varied interests.

My first meeting with Doctor Carrel took place at the Rockefeller Institute for Medical Research, where he headed the Department of Experimental Surgery. The friendship and collaboration resulting from that meeting took me often to his Breton island.

Carrel had the most stimulating mind I have known. His research in fields of biological life reached the limits of life and penetrated mysteries beyond. Generally, he worked within a conventional framework; but he refused to be imprisoned by it. Outside that framework, he could express himself with startling abandon. He might square his shoulders and assert that "all surgeons are butchers," and that "all people are fools," or he might sit contemplating at his desk and write that "on the scale of magnitudes, man exists midway between an atom and a star."

I was introduced to Carrel through a mutual friend, Doctor Paluel Flagg, an anaesthetist. The circumstances give insight to Carrel's character and standing, and to the status of surgery in 1930. They root into a family emergency.

My wife's older sister had developed a seriously defective heart valve as a complication of rheumatic fever. I had asked her doctor why surgery would not be beneficial. He replied that the heart could not be stopped long enough to permit a surgical operation. I asked why an artificial heart could not be used during the operation. He said he didn't know, and showed little interest in the problem. I asked other doctors. To my amazement, none of them could tell me, and none seemed to have much interest until I came to Paluel Flagg. He said that while he could not answer my questions, he had a friend who could—the French surgeon Alexis Carrel.

In his department and during lunch at the Rockefeller Institute, Carrel explained problems of coagulation, hemolysis, and infection. He said he had been trying for years to develop an apparatus similar to an artificial heart, one that would perfuse living organs isolated from the body. He showed me two mechanical devices that had been unsuccessful. I told him I thought I could construct a better perfusion apparatus. He replied that I would be welcome to the facilities of his department in the attempt to do so.

My original objective in working with Carrel was to develop a successful perfusion apparatus as a step toward an artificial heart. My interest in such an apparatus soon became secondary to my interest in Carrel himself and the elements of life he worked with. Since childhood, I had been fascinated by questions of life and death. How mechanical, how mystical was life? Did all existence end with death, or in some way extend beyond? Suppose an old head were grafted onto a young body, could wisdom and knowledge thus be combined with eternal youth? Carrel had explored all of these questions in his mind and laboratories, and both had become available to me.

I listened to Carrel discuss the causes of aging and the character of time, watched him transfusing blood from one dog to another, designed an experimental centrifuge-head that would let him replace the plasma of blood cells held in suspension, devised a quick method of obtaining serum in large quantities. I spent midnight hours with my microscope in the Department's incubator room studying living cells that had once composed a body. They could be kept alive forever in Carrel's culture flasks. Why, then, did the body they came from have to die? Since every body consisted of trillions of such individually-living cells, why should one think of oneself as an individual? But if man was not an individual, what was he?

The Rockefeller Institute concentrated attention scientifically on biological life, but Carrel's research invariably raised questions that extended far beyond the scope of biological science. His island of Saint Gildas, by its very nature, freed him of scientific bonds. To me, that island seemed created as a transition place between worldly life and universal spirit.

It is a small island. The Carrels ran it as a farm on peasant standards, pasturing several cows. Massive tides, ebbing and flowing through a range of forty feet, now separate it from, now connect it to the mainland. One may walk to it over the sea bottom, winding around weed-wet reefs and trapped pools containing shells, fish, and octopuses. One may return to it by boat across water that would float an ocean liner. Since there are times when one can neither walk nor cross by boat, life on the island is timed by tides as New York City life is timed by clocks.

Saint Gildas has a weird, austere, and kaleidoscopic beauty. Light, land, clouds, and ocean are never twice the same. The sun breaks through to warm the high-walled garden. The sea beats in to flood the inner marsh. At night, moonbeams may ghost with fog around big boulders or meteors streak through a star-bright sky.

It is easy to imagine sensing emanations from remains that mark thousands of years of human life. They come from the heavy, flat-rock dolmens, from a reputedly Roman wall, from foundations laid by monks of the Middle Ages, from the earth-floored church of the Saint himself. When storms rage, which they often do, waves dash so high upon the shore that island, air, and ocean seem to merge in a primeval chaos of which life, past and present, is a part.

In this environment, Carrel spent many summers of his life. Here he let his mind run free, contemplated mystical phenomena, and experimented with extrasensory perception. He was convinced that man has many powers of which he is consciously unaware, and that he extends beyond his body. He tried to find physical means of detecting this extension. Were subconscious faculties sometimes manifested by willow wands and pendulums? He and Madam Carrel spent hours with their friends experimenting with pendulums and averaging results. He was fascinated by a Breton contractor who would agree to dig a well at a price determined by a well diviner's estimate of the water-level depth. He was still more fascinated when the well diviner located with a pendulum a previously undiscovered dolmen ruin on Saint Gildas.

My close contacts with Carrel ended with his final return to France during World War II, but from the beginning of his professional career to his death in liberated Paris, his interests combined the physical and mystical. In 1941, under the Petain government, he organized and headed the Fondation Francaise pour l'etude des Problems Humains, whose mission was "to examine mechanical inventions, philosophic doctrines, modes of alimentation, methods of education, living habits, social and economic legislation, and so forth, from the point of view of their effects on the individual considered as an organic and spiritual whole."

During his last illness, Carrel said to his friend Dom Alexis of the Abbey of Boquen, "I pray that God will grant me another ten years of work. With what I have learned, and with what I have experienced, I believe I shall succeed in establishing, scientifically, certain objective relationships between the spiritual and the material, and thereby show the truth and beneficence of Christianity."

Doctor Edwards, in this perceptive and comprehensive biography, brings out the life, interests, accomplishments, and character of a great scientist and mystic. I believe his readers will find, as I did, that association with Alexis Carrel stimulates and broadens thought in an extraordinary way. (Tellina, Darien, Connecticut; December 29, 1973.)

CHARLES A. LINDBERGH

# PREFACE

"**I**F YOU THINK you've invented a new technique in heart or blood vessel surgery, you'd better check to see if Dr. Alexis Carrel didn't try the same thing 50 years ago."

Many young surgeons have heard this advice over the past twenty years as exciting new operations were being developed and methods found to save lives and limbs.

My interest in Carrel dates back to the mid 1950's when I was working in the early development of arterial grafts of cloth. It was astonishing to read Carrel's papers which were written in 1910 and watch his prophetic experiments become practical realities 40 years later.

Then in 1970, hoping to use biographical material relating to his life as the subject of an address, I found there had been no complete English biography written about this most remarkable man, and was stimulated to write this book.

I am deeply indebted to Robert Soupault, whose French biography of Carrel, published in 1950, was a major information source. Detailed information about Carrel's accomplishments during his long career in New York was obtained from *The History of the Rockefeller Institute* by George W. Corner. Thanks are due to Miss Margaret O'Byrne, Chief Librarian of Georgetown University Medical Library, and to Father Joseph Durkin, Custodian of the Carrel Collection, also at Georgetown. Mrs. Ruth Sternfelb, Assistant Librarian for Archives at Rockefeller University Library was very helpful. General and Mrs. Charles A. Lindbergh Jr. graciously supplied much interesting information about the Carrels.

Peter Edwards, my son, contributed greatly to the editing of the entire book and to the translation of much French material. He was also responsible for researching and writing the portions of the book dealing with the political problems encountered by Carrel.

W. Sterling Edwards M.D.
Albuquerque, New Mexico

# CONTENTS

ALEXIS CARREL

CHAPTER I

 EARLY YEARS

THE QUIET VILLAGE of Sainte-Foy-des Lyon is perched on one of the hills which overlooks the ancient city of Lyon in one of the oldest provinces of France. In the distance, the first Alpine foothills arise to the East and the Cevannes mountains to the South. The weathered roofs, the factory chimneys, the majestic confluence of the Rhone and the Soane rivers with their many bridges are below and sufficiently distant that the view may be enjoyed in silence. Here, on June 28, 1873, a boy was born who the next day was baptized Marie Joseph Auguste Carrel Billiard.

Carrel's ancestors had filled many high positions throughout the past three centuries in the service of Lyon and her institutions. His family was moderately wealthy, and has been characterized as "Provincial Catholic Upper class."

His father, Alexis Carrel Billiard, worked as a manufacturer of textiles; a small man, robust and jovial. In 1871, at 26, he had married the daughter of a linen merchant, Anne-Marie Ricard. The two families had been intimate for many years.

At their marriage, Anne-Marie was only nineteen years old. She was a highly attractive young woman with a tiny figure, her small face encircled by brown hair. A serious and intelligent person, she was endowed with an abundance of sensitivity and common sense.

Two years later, the couple's first child was born, and was given the name of his grandfather, Auguste. He was eighteen months old when his brother Joseph was born and three at the birth of his sister Marguerite.

The economy of France was booming in 1875, and the Carrel Billiard family blossomed. In the winter, the house on the embankment of the Rhone bustled with optimistic textile merchants, army officers and university intellectuals. The family passed the summers at the country home of Grandmother Ricard. Their life was comfortable and pleasant.

3

Monsieur Carrel Billiard had just finished plans to open a large factory in Alsace when in spite of good health, he developed pneumonia. A few days later he was dead. His widow, at 25, was left with the material and moral responsibility of raising three children.

For his first four years, the oldest son had been referred to as Bebe, but in memory of his father the family began to call him Alexis. For a time official documents referred to him as Auguste, but to his friends, schoolmates, and finally to the whole world he was simply Alexis Carrel.

With the death of the father, the family's economic prospects were altered drastically and removal to less expensive quarters became necessary. An apartment was obtained on the fourth floor of a house that faced the Soane. Much later, when recalling his early memories, Carrel mentioned that had the family become very rich, many things would have been spoiled since he believed the simplicity of bourgeois life in Lyon at that time to be an excellent contributor to the formation of good character.

Alexis was barely five when his father died, yet at that age he became the man of the house. He was made to understand that he was depended upon to be wise, obedient and punctual in the accomplishment of small daily tasks. Beside his brother and sister he didn't look much like the responsible man in the family, yet he felt the need to set an example and scolded them frequently when he deemed such disciplinary action to be necessary.

Madame Carrel, in the loneliness of her first few years of widowhood, was extremely comforted by her eldest son; he provided a bright light in her otherwise austere existence. Mother and son became very close, sharing each other's hopes and dreams as the years unfolded.

In the early years, her immediate concern, or entertainment as she called it, was the education of her children. Very early Alexis showed himself to be a curious observing type, and as a result was directed toward science. Joseph became interested in music, and later in musical criticism and composition. Marguerite was raised to be a wife and mother as were all middle class girls at that time.

In winter, the family lived within itself, studying many hours, taking walks or doing the many domestic chores. After a year of mourning the father, they began again to receive old friends and relatives. Thursdays and Sundays they dined three kilometers from their home with Grandmother Ricard and several uncles at Bellecours. They continued their habit of spending summers with Grandmother Ricard. From the beginning of May until the day for honoring the dead (All Saints Day), they escaped the gloomy apartment in town to the peace and beauty of the countryside.

At Grandmother Ricard's, the rambling building at the end of the garden had been converted into a laboratory for Uncle Joseph's experiments. Joseph, a 23 year old artillery lieutenant, seemed old and wise to his young nephew. Alexis watched in silent awe, and earned his right to observe by bringing water from the nearby stream which was always needed for his uncle's work.

Young Carrel took all of his early lessons at the St. Joseph day school conducted by Jesuit priests. He received his baccalaureate in letters in 1889, and in science in 1890. From the beginning, he was a serious student; independent, meditative and quiet. At times he was combative, possibly due to insecurity resulting from his small stature. On one occasion, to compliment him for having defended a friend in trouble, his teacher said to the principal within his hearing, "Alexis is no bigger than a mouse, but he is as brave as a lion." Instead of accepting the intended praise, Alexis felt only humiliation at being compared to a mouse. Out of vexation, he hid for several days.

Throughout these early years of study, he spent long hours in his mother's room discussing the events of the day and the next day's assignment. He arose early to work, a habit he continued all his life, and left for the daily mass at school by 7:30 in the morning. Though a conscientious student, Alexis' grades were good but not outstanding.

Carrel cared little for art, music or theater, although he did a little sketching later in his military service. Reading, on the other hand, constituted his favorite pastime.

He was a healthy boy, and was seldom ill. As physical exercise he took horseback lessons at a riding school. There were few organized sports in that era; vacations and weekends were spent flying kites, riding wooden wheeled bicycles or taking long walks in the country. From his youth he possessed a passionate love for nature. He once described his first revelation that occurred one summer day as he was dawdling through a field of wheat: "The top of the grain reached my nose and was like an immense deserted sea. Suddenly, floating capriciously over the moving surface, a butterfly sparkled with golden wings. I felt myself becoming a fabulous fairytale creature. An inexplicable emotion penetrated me, and from this poetic exchange was born the certainty that nature is not an abstract thing, but a living force, and that she offers to those who dare to question her the answer to many uncertainties."

In his adolescence, Alexis often dreamed of adventure in foreign lands, and seriously considered a career as an officer in the Colonial French Army. His nearsightedness, though he did not as yet wear glasses, would have prevented him from ever fulfilling this childhood fantasy.

At 17, he graduated from St. Joseph's and was faced with the necessity of choosing a career. A year of physics and natural sciences had excited his curiosity. He considered surgery, research, caring for patients. With little hesitation he decided to enter the Faculty of Medicine. This decision was totally unprecedented as no member of his family had previously practiced medicine.

He registered at the Faculty of Medicine in 1890, completed the courses and the practical work and after three years passed the final examinations. As was customary for those who chose to follow a hospital career, he then prepared for the hospital exams. He was accepted as an extern (number two out of fifty-seven applicants) on October 27, 1893. Carrel's next two years were spent at the Red Cross Hospital and the Hospital Antiguaille. In 1895, he served his one year of military service as a medical auxiliary in a unit of Chausseurs Alpins (mountain troops). The subsequent five years were spent completing an internship at several hospitals in Lyon, principally the Hotel Dieu.

His year in the Chausseurs Alpins was spent as a medical orderly and then as an assistant doctor to a small post in the high Alps on the Italian border. His unit consisted of twenty soldiers commanded by a lieutenant. Communication was often difficult, the life somewhat isolated. The bulk of the time was passed doing training exercises. Carrel was familiar with the use of skis, although they were uncommon in France at this time. He ordered a pair from Norway to facilitate his crossing the snow. The French army did not adopt skis for official use until several years later.

Despite the attachment that he had and always would have for his mother's profound faith, Carrel found his religious convictions playing an ever smaller role in the course of his life. Ten years he had submitted to Jesuit discipline, yet when he left the Jesuits, he did not revolt as did several of his friends. He simply accepted the principle of absolute objectivity that he had come to consider indispensable to both observation and the attainment of knowledge.

Alexis and his friends often discussed the metaphysical and current social problems pondered by most adolescents. They gathered one evening a week in the apartment of Adolphe Berthet, a charming, artistic young man who was to become a first rate scholar. In the group were Louis Aguettant, literature professor; Bonnevay, lawyer and future Minister of Justice; Francois Berthet, composer; and Paul Courmont, Joseph Germier, Pierre Prothon, Gignoux and Henri Moulin, all hospital interns. They discussed problems of aesthetics, ethics, surgery and medicine "with all of the fire and enthusiasm of youth." At these meetings Carrel behaved in his usual reserved manner, in contrast to the vehemence of some of his companions. He never failed to speak precisely and always employed rigorous reasoning. His correct demeanor and strict self discipline earned him the nickname *Guncotton* which was later shortened to just *Cotton*.

Among Alexis' acquaintances at this time was the medical student Marcel Rifaux who was to later write books causing a great uproar in early twentieth century bourgeois French society. On one occasion, Rifaux persuaded a group of fellow students to attend a controversial gathering of young radicals presided over by an infamous anarchist lecturer. So as to be inconspicuous, the young men were camouflaged as members of the proletariat sporting moth-eaten caps and worn vests. Carrel donned a flabby hat filled with newspaper to protect himself from the possibility of "knocks on the head." He brandished a large club in his right hand and a magnificent red belt was strapped about his waist. The true believers were not fooled for a moment, however, and the perpetrators of the charade were forced bodily to depart.

Young Carrel was somewhat particular in his style of dress. He had inherited a modest sum of money from his grandparents which allowed him to affect a careless elegance. He remained somewhat short, was of medium build, and under pince-nez possessed small, piercing eyes, one brown and one blue. This very rare physical peculiarity was hardly noticeable to those who knew him due to the thick glasses he wore for myopia. He was an amiable young man, but he could hardly be characterized as charitable. His intense, inner intellectual life left little time to think of others except when investigating them.

Carrel worked under a number of excellent teachers during his four years of internship. One, Poncet, dedicated his last fifteen years to the study of tuberculosis; another, Jaboulay, was the prestigious surgeon who had pioneered the suture of lacerated arteries. Ollier, a third, had advanced the study of physiology with his observations on the regeneration of bone. All three of these men considered the surgical act secondary in importance to the diagnosis and care of the patient. Nevertheless, from them Carrel became familiar with the most difficult and delicate operations as well as learning to diagnose disease, the indications for surgery and the methods of reducing the risk of operation.

In June, 1894, the assassination of the President of the French Republic, Sadi Carnot, in Lyon made a deep impression on Carrel, and provided him a forum for his unorthodox views of surgery. The predominant opinion was that since the fatal knife wound by the Italian anarchist had severed the portal vein, there was nothing surgeons could do to save the victim. Carrel insisted, however, that Carnot could have easily been saved if surgeons would only learn to sew up blood vessels as they sewed other tissues. Such sentiments by a young intern hardly endeared him to his surgical superiors who were not so forward-looking.

Two years later, learning about the first works of Jaboulay and his student, Briau, on vascular surgery, Alexis' attention was immediately attracted to this problem. Briau and Jaboulay had successfully united the ends of a divided carotid artery in the neck of a donkey by means of interrupted mattress (U shaped) sutures—so placed as to evert the edges of the vessel wall and approximate the inside layer, the intima. Carrel already realized the implications of being able to suture arteries and veins and the insufficiencies of the techniques employed.

At this time in history if a person sustained a laceration to an artery of an arm or leg, severe hemorrhage occurred with death resulting in a matter of minutes if the loss of blood was not stopped. Death could be prevented and hemorrhage stopped by tying the two cut ends of the torn artery with a piece of thread. If the injured artery lay between the heart and the elbow, or between the heart and the knee, it was very likely that the distant part of the extremity would not receive enough fresh blood to remain alive, and within a few hours or a day or two the extremity would turn black with gangrene. Amputation would then be required. Below the knee, and below the elbow, the major artery branches into two or three parallel arteries, so that any one of them can usually be ligated without danger of loss of the limb. Veins, the thin walled vessels which return the dark blood to the heart and lungs for more oxygen, are plentiful in the extremities and hemorrhage of veins can be controlled by ligature without danger to the limb. Loss of limbs from injuries to major arteries was a common occurrence in this era of duels with knife or sword, and especially in times of war. This was the stimulus for surgeons to search for techniques of repairing torn arteries rather than simply ligating them. About this time Payre developed some absorbable magnesium tubes which he used to connect the two ends of an artery, in experimental animals, but many of the arteries were occluded within a few days with blood clots. Between 1889 and 1900 several surgeons in Europe and America began to experiment with methods of sewing the two ends of arteries together with needle and thread. Jassinowski and Burci in Europe, Murphy in Chicago, and Briau and Jaboulay in Lyon were some of these pioneers. Most of these investigators emphasized the importance of confining the thread used for suturing to the outer vascular coats, believing that if the suture material

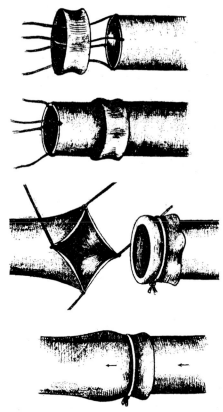

Figure 1. *Payre's Technique of Blood Vessel Anastamosis.* An absorbable ring of magnesium is threaded over the upstream (proximal) end of an artery, and the artery is cuffed back over the ring and tied. The cuffed artery and ring are then inserted into the distal arterial opening and tied. This was one of the earliest and simplest methods of joining two severed ends of a blood vessel. Unfortunately the blood frequently clotted after this anastamosis probably because of the internal irregularities inside the vessel at the junction point.

passed through the inner coat and came in contact with the blood flowing by, thrombosis (blood clotting) would be promoted. In 1899 Dorfler of Wissenberg, Germany, described the essentials of the method now so universally and successfully employed for artery repair, the principle features being the employment of fine round needles and fine silk, and continuous sutures embracing all of the coats of the vessels. He observed that the presence of

Figure 2. *Briau and Jaboulay's Method of Direct End-to-End Union of Blood Vessels.* Here an effort was made to join together two ends with a minimal amount of suture material exposed to the flowing blood, and by everting the lips of the vessel, minimizing any possibility of flaps of the cut edges protruding into the blood stream to produce clotting. This worked well, but required considerable dexterity on small vessels and also necessitated handling the cut vessel ends with forceps.

an aseptic (sterile) thread in the lumen of a vessel did not necessarily lead to changes which might interfere with its remaining open and functioning. In fact, he recommended that all coats be included in the continuous suture. Carrel knew about the work of Briau and Jaboulay, but it is not known if he was aware of some of the other work. Communication of scientific advances was slower and more erratic in that era than now.

Carrel sought laboratory space where he could execute his experiments and he found such space first under Auguste Lumiere, then in the laboratory of Marcel Soulier, a venerable professor of therapeutics, whose son was his close friend. Here Alexis worked with complete freedom for many semesters. He became more and more successful in suturing vessels as he gained experience. He discouraged all but his close friends from watching him work but his success became known locally and great speculations began to arise in conversations and in local medical journals as to the potential applications of vascular anastomosis in humans. One of the most intriguing possibilities that was frequently discussed was the transplantation of entire organs from one individual to another. Carrel did not contribute to this speculation but the commentaries continued and in one of the most

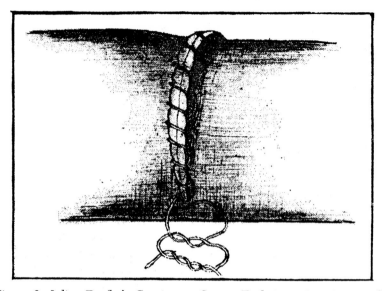

Figure 3. *Julius Dorfler's Continuous Suture Technique.* In 1899 Dorfler convincingly demonstrated that if small round needles and fine silk suture were used, it did not matter if the thread was exposed to the blood stream. He used an over-and-over continuous suture through all layers, but this method also was tedious and required picking up the cut ends with forceps for each suture. This resulted in bruising of the delicate vessel ends which increased the tendency to occlusion from clotting.

prominent medical journals the famous professor of physiology, Morat, wrote that transplantation of certain visceral organs, such as the kidney, of one animal to another did not have much chance of success as long as it was impossible to connect the vasomotor nerves. The first attempt at suturing the end of an artery to the end of a vein was made by Bernard and Carrel in the laboratory of Auguste Lumiere. "The femoral artery and saphenous vein of a large dog were exposed in Scarpa's triangle and the central end of the artery was united to the peripheral end of the vein. The red blood was made to flow through the vein which as a result was distended, pulsated, and exhibited the main arterial characteristics. The anastomosis adequately withstood the arterial blood pressure but no long term results were observed as the animal died from infection two days after the operation."

Afterwards, several other experiments were performed by

Carrel and Morel in the laboratory of Professor Soulier. The first dog operated on made a good recovery but eight days after the operation, the vessel was found to be occluded by a fibrous clot. The next experiment was entirely successful. The external jugular vein in the neck of a dog was dissected and cut and its peripheral end united to the central end of the carotid artery. The arterial circulation through the vein was very active. Several weeks after the operation, this animal was presented before the Societé Nationale de Medecine, at which time the external jugular vein pulsated like an artery. By listening over the neck with a stethoscope, a strong murmur could be heard at the point of anastomosis. During the several months the animal was under observation the results remained satisfactory. Jaboulay was present and commented that this kind of arterovenous anastomosis of the vessels to and from the brain might improve the circulation to the brain in patients with insufficient circulation, as in cerebral softening.

It was necessary to find very fine needles and thread to accomplish the anastomosis of arteries and veins. The manufacturers of surgical instruments were not able to help as they did not have these small sizes available. Carrel discovered from his mother that he might be able to find these objects at the wholesale haberdashery of Messieurs Assada, known to all the people of Lyon. These men were able to fulfill his request with the needles and thread of a lace woman. It is not known whether this was cotton, linen or silk thread, but with this material he was able to start the work that was to make him famous. As time went by, he acquired even greater manual dexterity which always impressed those who watched him operate, both in the United States and in France. He attributed this dexterity to the instruction he received from an embroidress of renown in Lyon, Mme. Leroudier, who gave him embroidery lessons at her home during his internship. Alexis was occasionally teased about his needlework, but he did not attempt to defend himself, nor did he enter into the arguments about the therapeutic implications of his work.

These experiments were done at odd hours and did not interfere with his hospital work or his preparation for exams.

One of his chores as an intern between 1898 and 1900 was to

give lectures to a group of younger students still in medical school. This was an effective teaching-learning experience if the lecturer was knowledgeable and talented. It was valuable because the teacher and students were close to the same age and were, therefore, freer to argue with each other. This was generally not true when the age difference was greater. Among Carrel's students was Rene Leriche, who was to become a brilliant and famous Professor of Surgery with a primary interest in the circulation. Carrel was, from the beginning of their association, impressed with the sharp intelligence of Leriche, and a sincere and durable friendship developed between them.

During this time Carrel, under Professor Poncet, was preparing his doctoral thesis on cancer of the thyroid. It was a very well documented monograph, very much to the point. It was completed and accepted in 1901 and he received a number of complimentary remarks on it from his peers. This same year, as an intern, he took his clinical exam for a position on the surgical staff under Poncet but the brilliant Vignard won this position. This first failure was accepted without bitterness, but Carrel worked with little spirit through the narrow, slow, and winding channels which led to a hospital surgical post at that time. It took him another two years to catch up with his friend Vignard and to gain a staff position for himself.

After Vignard's appointment, Carrel took a very difficult surgical exam at the hospital. To prepare for this exam, which many talented students failed on their first or second attempt, he spent many long nocturnal hours after the labor of a full day. There was little leisure during this period for meditation or creative thought.

For amusement and to break the monotony of cramming for this exam, he decided to join his friend Emile Gallois in a small welfare center especially designed for industrial injuries. Here he dedicated himself to the study of trauma, giving free reign to his ability. This was characteristic of his approach to a new field of interest; Alexis jumped in full of enthusiasm to learn all he could.

In 1900, Madame Carrel rented by the year a small chateau in the countryside near Lyon in the area called Saint-Martin-en-Haut. This chateau was called "La Batie," and was perched on the side of a hill in the middle of great wooded country. Her son loved to visit her there every Sunday during the summer months, travelling by means of a gasoline fueled tricycle. He spent a part of each annual vacation at La Batie until 1942.

Alexis Carrel had arrived at the age of thirty, with no financial worries, treasured and guided by the most attentive of mothers, appreciated by his superiors, and admired by his colleagues. Several important character traits were by now well established. He possessed an innate curiosity which increased with the years. Medicine and surgery, in which he had been trained, could provide a great feast for his intellectual appetite if only he were allowed the freedom to follow his interests. He did not procrastinate, nor compromise. He had the courage of his convictions, and could even be foolhardy, if necessary. He was not unsociable, but distant. The word that would perhaps describe him best is "intense."

As Carrel appraised his situation, he found himself surrounded by a Lyonaise society with narrow, provincial ideas, which ignored or actively resisted change, was critical of all originality and rejected all desire for independence. He developed a disgust for politicians that remained with him throughout his life. In medicine, as well, there existed an attitude of conformity to the point of stagnation. The Chief of Staff of each hospital and each department established protocol and procedures and no innovations were sanctioned. Alexis became more and more depressed by the small-minded goals and the financial ambitions of the surgeons of his acquaintance. He felt himself smothered by this oppressive atmosphere. Many long hours were spent with his mother discussing these inner conflicts.

An interesting event occurred at about this time which influenced his future. A group of young missionaries, before leaving for the extreme northern part of Canada, came to ask the young surgeon to instruct them in emergency surgery. He provided them with several lectures and demonstrations at Hôtel Dieu. Impressed by his skill and knowledge, they begged him to accompany them to Canada and to share in her treasures. The fantasy of adventure aroused by this invitation intrigued Carrel, for he had dreamed more than once of exploring an unknown country.

The conditions were right for such a move. However, he found himself unable at the moment to renounce his country, the dear presence of home, mother and friends. A seed was planted, and no doubt slowly germinated.

For the second time he prepared for the difficult surgical exam; again he failed. His failure was not too surprising, since almost all the candidates took the exam three or four times before finally passing. Alexis was not one to lament. On the contrary, he immediately accepted the challenge, at the cost of becoming even more intense, distant and easily irritated.

# CHAPTER II

# THE MIRACLE AT LOURDES

IN MAY, 1903, Carrel accepted an invitation from the priest in charge of the yearly pilgrimage at Lourdes to travel with the "sick train" and observe the alleged miracle cures first hand. As a scientist and faculty member of the medical school at Lyon, he had been attracted by the stories of the cures at Lourdes and relished the opportunity to check their authenticity. No systematic study of this phenomena had as yet been undertaken, and Carrel eagerly accepted the opportunity to "examine the facts objectively, just as a patient is examined at a hospital or an experiment conducted in a laboratory."

As the train departed the station at Lyon, Carrel settled down in the compartment marked "Management." He seated himself next to the priest in charge of the train, and inquired as to the possibility that some of its passengers might be cured.

"The Holy Virgin has always accorded us great favor," responded the priest. "Out of every three hundred patients, some 50 or 60 always feel they have improved or been cured."

"And what about all those who hope for a cure and suffer the miseries of a long journey in vain?", asked Carrel.

"You are reckoning without faith, my dear doctor. Those who are not cured come back comforted, and even if they die when they get home, they are still happy."

Carrel began to classify the few observations of the sick he had already made, and started to review the case histories of the rest given him by the priest. After a few hours, he drifted off to sleep.

At six the next morning, he arose and began to make rounds of the patients on the train. In a third class compartment he came upon a young girl lying prone on a mattress stretched across two benches. Her name, he discovered, was Marie Bailly.

"I am suffering a great deal," she told Doctor Carrel, "but I am happy I came. The sisters did not want me to leave Lyon."

Carrel promised the girl that he would return to see her that evening, and told her to call the nurse for an injection if the pain became worse. He commented to a second priest that the girl was indeed gravely ill, and asked that he make the necessary preparations in the event that she should die before reaching her destination at Lourdes. Marie's belly was distended, the skin stretched tightly, and at the sides her ribs protruded sharply. The swelling seemed to be caused by solid masses, and a pocket of fluid was found under the umbilicus. Her legs were swollen and her temperature above normal. Both heartbeat and breathing were accelerated. Without doubt, she suffered from tuberculous peritonitis.

The nun who had brought Mlle. Bailly to the train had informed Carrel that she had been sick all of her life, and that both of her parents had died from the same disease. A few days before the pilgrimage was to begin her doctors had considered operating, but had declined because the chief surgeon believed her condition "too precarious." Her family was told that her case was hopeless. She begged to be permitted to make the pilgrimage to Lourdes, and because the doctors could do nothing more for her, they had finally given their consent.

Carrel injected a shot of morphine into Marie's emaciated arm; it eased her pain and after a few hours she was asleep. She slept through the night, and remained unconscious as the train pulled into Lourdes at two o'clock the next afternoon. Carrel later wrote, "The train had reached the holy land, the city of miracles, the goal of this long and bitter journey—Lourdes itself. From every window pale faces looked out, alight with joy and exaltation, to greet the chosen land where their misfortunes were to vanish like the wind. No one spoke. Everyone was gazing towards the basilica where each private prayer might be miraculously answered."

At noon the next day Carrel left his hotel to inspect the famous grotto where so many miracles were supposed to have occurred. Among the many volunteers Carrel recognized an old classmate, and together they decided to observe the immersion of the patients into the pools which was to begin at half past one. Carrel inquired of his friend if any patients had been cured that morning to which the volunteer replied that he himself had witnessed a miracle.

"An old nun, as a result of a sprain six months ago, had developed an incurable disease in her foot. She was cured and threw aside her crutches."

Carrel reflected a moment and responded, "Isn't that the nun who was a nurse at the Hotel Dieu in Lyon?"

"Yes, that's the one," answered his friend.

"Well, her cure is an interesting example of auto suggestion. She happens to be one of the patients I examined. Her sprained foot was completely well, but she persuaded herself that she would never walk normally again. She had become neurasthentic. She came to Lourdes and she was cured. What could be more natural?"

"But how do you explain that Lourdes succeeded in curing her when other treatment failed?"

"Because," answered Carrel, "there is an incredible power of suggestion at a pilgrimage. A crowd exalted and united by prayer can have a tremendous effect on the nervous system, but absolutely no effect on organic disease."

"Just the same," his friend replied, "I assure you that real organic diseases such as tumors can disappear. But you cannot believe it because you are convinced that miracles are impossible. Yet it lies entirely within God's power to suspend the laws of nature since it was He himself who created them."

"Of course," said Carrel, "if God exists, miracles are possible. But does God exist, objectively? How am I to know? All I can say is that no miracle has ever yet been scientifically observed. To the scientific mind a miracle is an absurdity. There is one terminally ill patient, however," Carrel continued, "whom I have been watching with great care. Her name is Marie Bailly. If such a case as hers were cured, it would indeed be a miracle. I would never doubt again."

It was almost two when Carrel arrived at the pools. The patients were not yet there. Carrel seated himself at the door by the women's pool, and a few minutes later his friend and another volunteer appeared carrying Marie Bailly on a stretcher.

Just before going to the pool, they brought her to Doctor

Carrel who immediately checked her pulse. It was more rapid than ever. She was unconscious; her face deathly white. Carrel warned his companions that she was on the verge of death. They decided that the danger of immersing her into the pool was too great, and that they should only sprinkle a bit of water upon her stomach. This was immediately done with no noticeable results.

By two thirty, Marie's respiration had become less rapid; the doctors assumed this to be a sign that she was about to die. Suddenly the blanket covering her distended abdomen began to flatten. They believed the folds in the blanket to be playing tricks on them, but a few minutes later her belly was completely flat. The heartbeat, though still very rapid, had become regular. She had regained consciousness and in answer to the doctors' questions said that she felt well, although still weak, and that she believed that she was cured. The Mother Superior offered her a glass of milk; she drank it all. She raised her head, turned on her side and seemed to be in no pain whatsoever.

Carrel was totally dumbfounded, but not completely convinced. At half past seven that evening he went to the girl's hospital room to insure that the girl's recovery was real, and that he had not dreamed the events of the preceding afternoon. He later noted, "The change was overpowering. Marie Bailly, in a white jacket, was sitting up in bed. Though her face was still grey and emaciated, it was alight with life. Her eyes shone; a faint color tinged her cheeks. Such an indescribable serenity emanated from her person that it seemed to illuminate the whole sad ward with joy." Her pulse was calm and regular, her respiration completely normal. He examined her stomach which remained absolutely flat. There was not a trace of the distention and hard masses that had been there before. That same year, Marie Bailly entered the religious service of the Daughters of Charity at St. Vincent de Paul, where she remained until her death at fifty-one years of age on February 22, 1937.

This inexplicable experience completely mystified Carrel, but he resolved not to shirk his responsibilities, and dutifully reported his findings to the medical community in Lyon. In addition, he candidly responded to all queries of the press. Due to his already considerable medical reputation, his observations were headlined in newspapers throughout France. Ironically, he was attacked on the one hand by the clergy for being overly skeptical, and on the other by organized medicine for being "gullible." One of his superiors warned, "My friend, with your ideas you would do better to renounce the concours (the very important surgical exams). You will never pass them now." This admonition undoubtedly played a large part in Carrel's decision to leave France.

In spite of the certainty that he should leave, Alexis was uncertain as to where he should go. He and his mother discussed his future at great length. It was unusual for professional men to become expatriates. Where could he pursue his profession? In another Faculty in France? Impossible. In the colonies? Perhaps. Or should he renounce medicine altogether? He would then lose the benefit of twelve years of education and effort, and the development of so much talent. Finally he decided to give up clinical medicine, and to concentrate his efforts on research.

Immediately following the incident at Lourdes Carrel left on his first trip to Paris, where he remained from December 1903 to March 1904. He took an inexpensive room in a small hotel. He no longer frequented surgical wards; they no longer interested him. Instead, he attended lectures in history, art and music. He listened to Jules Soury, who lectured with closed eyes on cerebral physiology. No doubt he spent much time reflecting upon the future course of his life.

He returned to Lyon in March and left for Canada on the first of May. Canada was considered the France of America, a country of adventure, of the future. Canada possessed immense expanses of farm and ranchland. When questioned years later, Carrel maintained that at the time of his departure from France he planned to renounce medicine completely and take up ranching.

# CHAPTER III

 NEW LIFE IN AMERICA

THE PREPARATION FOR his long voyage took place in secret. No one was told of it except Alexis' sister and brother-in-law. He told neither his grandmother, his intimate friends nor his former professors.

Carrel left Lyon on May 6, 1904, promising his mother to see her soon in France or America, but they were never to see each other again. The ship sailed from Bordeaux, and after fourteen violent days at sea, docked at Quebec. Alexis continued on to Montreal, obtained a room in a boarding house run by an old French lady, and the following morning, despite rainy weather, began to explore the city on foot. He stopped in front of a large and beautiful building. A policeman informed him that this was the Hotel Dieu, the great Catholic Hospital. He went inside and casually visited the wards, nodding to the patients without saying a word. He observed with great interest the patient and silent work of the Sisters of Charity dressed in grey. A young doctor with a short blonde mustache approached him.

"May I help you?"

Carrel responded with several words of bad English mixed with French.

"But you are French! Who brought you here? May I know your name?"

"Of course, my name is Alexis Carrel."

"Oh, are you related to the scholar-author of experimental research at Lyon?"

"It's me."

In this way Carrel became acquainted with Francois de Martigny who in turn introduced him to his brother, Adelstan, already a well known doctor in Montreal. The Martigny brothers invited him to dinner, welcomed him on their hospital services and introduced him to Montreal society. They persuaded him to remain in town for a few weeks to become more familiar with the language and customs. The friendship that evolved lasted many years.

At the beginning of July he attended the Second Medical Congress of the French Language of North America at Montreal and presented a paper on vascular anastamosis, describing the operating technique and indications. It caused a sensation. Among those attending the Congress were several American surgeons. Dr. Karl Beck and his brother, both from Chicago, conversed at length with him and discussed the possibility of his coming to work in Chicago. The Martigny brothers attempted to persuade him to remain and work with them in Montreal. During his two month stay he wrote an article with Adelstan de Martigny describing a bandage that de Martigny had invented. This article was published in *Lyon Medicine.*

Carrel left Montreal August 10, 1904 to travel by train across Canada to the west coast, then down to San Francisco and back across the United States. He wrote extensive notes during his hours on the train.

"Dress doesn't mean anything. If a man introduces himself, they listen and even ask him questions. If he is uninteresting or dull, they abandon him. If he has a value, they hold on to him and use him. Friendships and recommendations are of no value. Here, from infancy they tell their children that they can do anything they wish, that even if they lose their money, they can still make another fortune. In our country parents tell children they must obtain a station in life, get themselves recommendations; that if they lose their station or their money, it is a dreadful thing; life is ruined. It is heart-breaking and distressing for a Frenchman who loves his country and who is perceptive to look around and to notice this original inferiority."

In Winnipeg he visited Dr. Dubrec, a former laborer, a self made physician who practiced surgery according to the books without having ever seen an operation.

Crossing Alberta, Alexis wrote: "The wheat fields become more rare. It's a dry prairie, an immense yellow tapestry all the way up to the horizon. The slightest details of the landscape are vigorously etched. There are some very strange animals. Strong bulls (buffaloes?) are galloping heavily toward us. Darker hues mark swamps and mud holes. The infinite countryside appears almost deserted. Every now and then there are some cabins. Night is falling. The depots are simple wooden buildings. The train is stopping. A man gets off—alone—he goes off toward some ranch lost in the prairie!"

In Calgary he visited a priest who struck him as "a fairly nice man, but with limited intelligence. There should be enough candidates for the priesthood to be able to make a choice. On the subject of colonization, too, he is very imprecise and vague. He sees fairly clearly the affairs of France. He angered me by his desire to get money and the low ways he employed to get it. I told him that Combes was the great reformer of the Catholic Church, and that he would force priests into poverty. He was very shocked. Lord! how is it that men who each day eat your flesh and drink your blood are so far from your spirit?"

He briefly visited Vancouver, San Francisco, and Los Angeles, and arrived in Chicago in late September, disenchanted with his future as a rancher.

Chicago first impressed Alexis as "The big dirty city. Heart rending impression is the crowdedness, the crisis, the feverish activity of the crowds. Michigan Avenue, the Lake, the big boulevards, the intersections. The terrible noise of the elevated Metro, the underground tramways. And then the mud, the dirtiness of the streets. The traffic, the big stores, high buildings. The gray sky, the dirty clouds, the heat and humidity."

He spent his first two months becoming familiar with Chicago, and improving his English. He visited Professor Webster whom he had first met in Montreal. He became acquainted with Professor Murphy, the "Dean" of American surgery, and with Emmanual W. Senn and Wagner. He was asked to give surgical lectures. In November 1904 he was offered two positions, one at the University of Illinois under Dr. Karl Beck, and another in the Hull Laboratory of Physiology at the University of Chicago under Dr. George N. Stewart. He accepted the latter position and was assigned to work with Dr. Charles C. Guthrie. Between November 1904 and August 1906 they jointly wrote twenty-one papers. Their relationship was an interesting one. Carrel was then 31, Guthrie was 25 and only four years out of medical school.

Carrel was quite dependent on Guthrie to help with his writing and speaking since his English was not yet fluent. Carrel supplied the bulk of the imagination and energy, and performed most of the experiments. Guthrie was away from Chicago from February to December 1905 on Sabbatical leave at the University of Missouri. They corresponded frequently during this period. In a letter from Carrel to Guthrie dated December 10, 1905, Carrel asked Guthrie to write a speech for him to give at a Physiology meeting in Ann Arbor, Michigan. "I do not wish to speak more than five or eight minutes on account of my bad pronunciation."

The first accomplishment was the development of a laboratory which would allow animal operations to be done under aseptic condition. Carrel's previous experiments in Lyon were terminated after several hours or a few days by infection which caused either thrombosis of the anastomosis or death of the animal.

Next, the technique of vascular anastomosis was perfected. In Lyon, Carrel had been careful to avoid penetrating the inner layer with suture when performing vascular anastomosis, believing that sutures exposed to the blood promoted clotting. This effort was now abandoned and all layers of the vessel wall were included.

A third major advance was the development of the triangulation method of anastomosis which today bears Carrel's name. The two ends of the vessels to be sutured were first approximated by three separate sutures spaced one third of the way around the circumference. Retraction on each of these sutures held the vessel ends together for easy insertion of a continuous stich and avoided the possibility of catching the back wall of the artery inadvertently. Prior to this time surgeons customarily picked up the edges of the cut end of the vessel with forceps to make each stitch. This resulted in bruising and swelling of the vessel wall which interfered with its healing.

Both men continued to search for finer needles and thread. Guthrie sent Carrel some silk threads taken from the ravelings from a silk flour bolting cloth which he obtained from a miller in Columbia. Carrel excitedly wrote, "Your silk is splendid. Take a lot of it, as we are going to use only that kind of thread."

Another project was to consider again the problem of suturing arteries to veins. No one had been able to successfully perform

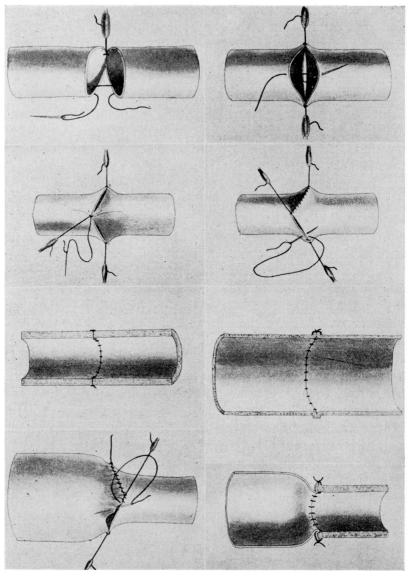

Figure 4. *Carrel's Triangulation Technique.* These diagrams show his now famous method which greatly simplified and made safer the anastamosis of vessels. Each of three simple sutures is placed through the cut ends approximately one third the way around the circumference of the anastomosis. With an assistant applying gentle tension on these three sutures, the edges of the vessels can be lined up in such a way that the surgeon can rapidly

an arterio-venous anastomosis prior to Carrel's work in Lyon in 1902. Now many experiments were performed suturing arteries to veins in dogs. The carotid artery was anastomosed to the jugular vein in the neck, and the femoral artery to the femoral vein in the leg. In some experiments the proximal artery was sutured to the distal vein and in other animals this was reversed. Carrel and Guthrie clearly demonstrated for the first time that veins could tolerate the higher pressure that exists in arteries. Reversal of flow was shown to be possible in veins, in spite of the presence of venous valves; the valves gave way under the force and velocity of arterial blood pressure.

In other experiments, grafting of a segment of fresh vein into an artery was shown to be practical. Under the microscope, weeks or months after operation, veins grafted into arteries show thickened walls to compensate for the higher pressure. The discrepancy in size between the smaller artery and larger vein was found to have become adjusted, at least at the point of anastamosis, and the suture line had healed smoothly on the inside. Patch grafts made of veins to enlarge the inside diameter of arteries were described for the first time and were shown to be quite satisfactory. Today it seems amazing that these techniques did not see clinical application for forty years, until after World War II. This was primarily because the danger of infection in traumatic wounds prevented the use of arterial reconstructions including replacement of damaged arterial segments with vein grafts. Carrel correctly predicted that vein grafts would be useful one day in the replacement of popliteal aneurysms (dangerous dilated arteries behind the knee). It is surprising that some bold surgeon did not attempt this form of therapy before the 1950's since this procedure can be done cleanly and not as an emergency.

run a continuous over-and-over suture across each intervening section, with almost perfect opposition and no need to handle the arteries with forceps. The third pair of diagrams shows how smoothly the inner layers are approximated by this technique, with no projecting edges. The lower left panel shows how a large vein can be anastamosed to a smaller artery, by advancing slightly further with each suture on the vein side than on the arterial side.

Figure 5. *Vein Graft to Replace a Segment of Artery.* Since veins of the body are much more plentiful and expendable than arteries, Carrel and Guthrie carried out many experiments using both fresh and preserved veins to replace excised segments of arteries. The thinner vein wall became slightly thicker after several months, due to the higher arterial pressure to which it was subjected.

Carrel and Guthrie believed that a recently amputated limb could be saved by quickly sewing its vessels back together. To prove this they amputated completely and immediately re-implanted the hind leg of a dog. They divided and then re-attached all structures including muscle, bone, blood vessels and nerves. The circulation was re-established after having been interrupted for one and one quarter hours.

"Seven days after the operation the dressing was partly re-moved. The limb presented neither edema (swelling) nor trophic troubles (dead tissue). The skin was normal and the wound had united 'per primam intentionem' without evidence of inflammation. The temperature of the skin was higher below than above the suture line."

"On the tenth day, during the afternoon, the temperature of the replanted foot became lower, i.e. similar to the normal foot. The dressing was then removed. It was found that, owing to a slipping of the plaster bandage, some urine had got into the cotton dressing and caused infection of the upper part of the longitudinal incision. A small subcutaneous abcess had developed along the vessels. The general condition of the animal was excellent and the nutrition of the limb satisfactory. As the arterial pulsations were much weakened and as it was considered important to accurately determine the cause of this change, the animal was etherized and the vessels examined through cutaneous incisions, after which the animal was killed. This examination revealed that the vascular anastomoses were surrounded by the subcutaneous abcesses and that the arterial anastomosis was partially occluded by a small clot." Thus again infection caused thrombosis and failure of the otherwise satisfactory experiment. No mention at this time was made of the neurological status of the replanted limb, or whether there was any return of sensation or motion. The first human limb replantation was performed in 1962 at the Massachusetts General Hospital in Boston when the arm of a 12 year old boy was successfully replanted after having been completely amputated just below the shoulder by a train. Using Carrel and Guthrie's techniques outlined forty years before, the vessels, nerves, and bones were successfully reattached.

Kidney transplantation was the next problem to be investigated. In Lyon in 1902 Carrel had transplanted one kidney of a dog from its abdomen to its neck. The renal (kidney) artery and veins were sutured to the carotid and jugular vessels and the end of the ureter (the small tube that carries urine from the kidney to bladder) was united to a small opening of the skin of the neck. On release of the clamps, the circulation was immediately re-established and seemed thoroughly normal. After a few hours clear fluid began flowing from the ureter. The animal died in a few days from infection.

In the same year, 1902, unknown to Carrel, Ullman also removed and transplanted a dog's kidney to the neck, uniting the renal and carotid artery and the renal and external jugular veins by Payr's method of absorbable rings. The kidney secreted urine for a time after the operation but early thrombosis occurred. In 1903 the same experiment was performed in Chicago by Dr. Karl Beck, but was not published.

In 1905 Floresco from Bucarest reported the results of numerous renal grafting procedures in animals which he began in 1902. He used circular suture technique, which he credited to Carrel. He recommended transplanting the kidney into the lower abdomen and implanting the ureter into the bladder. This is now the technique used in human kidney transplants. One of his animals lived for more than a month. He tested various methods of preventing coagulation in the vessels of kidneys during grafting procedures, such as the injection of salt solutions to displace the blood, and the injection of peptone solutions and solutions of leech extract into the general circulation prior to the operation.

Carrel and Guthrie worked in the Hull Laboratory in perfecting their technique of renal transplantation to the neck and reported the results of function of such a kidney three days after transplantation. "The circulation in the transplanted kidney was slightly greater than in the normal kidney, as detected by the touch, copiousness of hemorrhage from incision in cortex, and pulse tracings. The secretion of urine by the transplanted kidney was about five times more rapid than by the normal one. The intravenous injection of sodium chloride solution caused no change in the rate of secretion of the normal but markedly increased the rate of secretion in the transplanted organ."

A method of kidney transplantation in mass was developed by

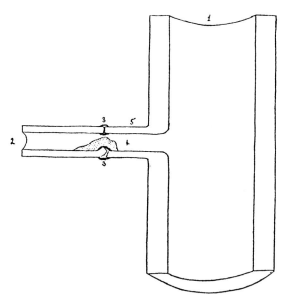

Figure 6. *Carrel's Patch Method of Blood Vessel Anastomosis Used Especially in Kidney Transplantation.* The earliest method of connecting the renal vessels of the donor kidney to the recipients circulation was to perform end-to-end anastomosis between the two small renal arteries. In dogs these vessels are about half the size of a lead pencil and if there is any imperfection or irregularity at all at the junction, a clot will form and the transplanted kidney will die.

Carrel and Guthrie in which the organs were permitted to retain their normal connections with a portion of their nervous apparatus, in such a manner that after transplantation their functions would hopefully soon be re-established. Both kidneys, the upper part of the ureter, the renal vessels, and a short segment of the aorta and vena cava from which the renal vessels took origin were removed from one animal and implanted in another. The circulation was re-established after having been interrupted for one hour and a half. The kidneys immediately became red and turgid, as after simple transplantation, but about half an hour later the state of the circulation became normal. Clear urine flowed abundantly from the transplanted ureters which were united to the normal ones. Both normal kidneys were dissected and extirpated.

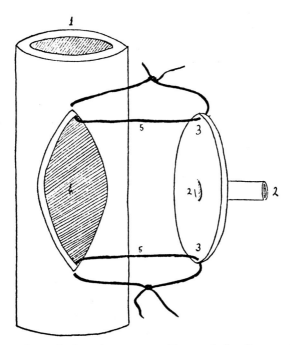

Figure 7. *Patch Method of Anastomosis.* To avoid the dangers inherent in a small vessel anastomosis, Carrel removed a button or patch of the wall of the aorta containing the mouth of the renal artery when he removed a kidney from the donor animal. He then excised a similar button of tissue from the wall of the aorta of the recipient animal and sutured the donor patch in place.

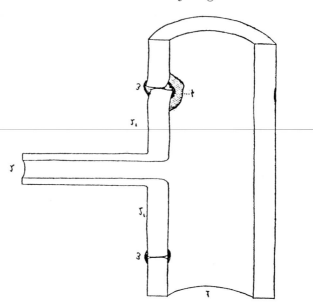

Figure 8. *Patch Method of Anastomosis.* When the patch was anastomosed to the aorta, any irregularity resulting in the formation of a small clot would be well away from the renal artery opening.

This animal did well for two weeks before he died from kidney failure. This experiment was repeated several times and survivals of "several weeks" were obtained which was longer than any survivals reported to that time. Carrel and Guthrie did not appreciate the importance of rejection in their transplants of organs between different animals of the same species (homografts). Carrel makes the following statement in a paper written during this time:

"The ordinary surgical methods of blood-vessel anastomosis have failed to give successful results in the transplantation of organs. At first I used tubes of magnesium or tubes of "caramel" but without good results. Coagulation occurred. Afterward I found a method of suturing which was often successful. By degrees that method has been improved in such a manner that now obliteration almost never occurs. Dr. Guthrie and I, operating together, obtain practically constantly good results. That very important question of technique being settled, autotransplantation (same animal) and homotransplantation (same species) become almost easy. The problem of heterotransplantation (different species) is much more complicated. It is well known that the serum of an animal in many cases is toxic for the cells of an animal of another species. The aim of these researches being to determine the possibility of transplanting organs from animal to man, that question is very important. Fortunately, biologic laws are not without exceptions. Perhaps the human serum is not toxic for the cells of some animals. We have some reason to think that organs of the anthropoid apes transplanted on man may not be injured by the serum, for the blood of ape and man are inactive toward each other. Besides, it might be possible to use anticytolytic serums. All these points are unknown and must be experimentally studied."

This statement by Carrel suggests that he thought that organs transplanted between animals of the same species (homotransplants) would not undergo rejection, as would organs transplanted between two animals of different species (heterotransplants).

Transplantation experiments were attempted using ovaries and thyroid. To transplant ovaries the method of transplantation in mass was used. In cats, the ovary, the ovarian artery and a portion of the aorta and vena cava corresponding to the mouth of the ovarian artery and vein were cut by proper incisions. The Fallopian tube is severed near its fimbriated end. These structures were sutured to the appropriate areas in another cat after removing the ovary and its blood supply. These experiments were interesting only from a technical point of view since there was no way to test the function of the ovary. The authors state: "Our experiments were performed on ordinary laboratory animals of uncertain breeds. We intend to very soon perform a series of similar operations on pure bred animals, preferably dogs and pigs, with a view of studying the problem of transmission of characters and related problems."

The thyroid gland was extirpated and replanted with reversal of the circulation. Eleven days after the operation the wound was opened and the gland was found to have a good circulation. Even after 94 days the systolic pulsation of the gland could still be felt. This also was only of technical interest since the function of this thyroid graft was not tested. The ultimate goal for a thyroid graft with reversal of its circulation was the hope that this might prove to be an effective means of treating hyperthyroidism. Thyroid transplantation had never before been successful. Carrel's original attempt in Lyon had failed in a few hours due to thrombosis of the vascular anastomoses.

Even the heart did not escape the efforts of these two investigators. "The heart of a small dog was extirpated and transplanted into the neck of a larger one by anastamosing the cut ends of the jugular vein and the carotid artery to the aorta, the pulmonary artery. The circulation was re-established through the heart about an hour and 15 minutes after the cessation of the heartbeat. Twenty minutes after the re-establishment of the circulation the blood was actively circulating through the coronary system. A small opening being made through the wall of a small branch of the coronary vein, an abundant dark hemorrhage was produced. Then strong fibrillar contractions were seen. Afterward contractions of the auricles appeared, and about an hour after the operation, effective contractions of the ventricles began." The transplanted heartbeat at the rate of 88 per minute, while the rate of the normal heart was 100 per minute. Owing to the fact that the operation was made without aseptic technique, coagulation occurred in the cavities of the heart after about two hours, and the experiment was interrupted.

In April 1905 Carrel was invited by Harvey Cushing to give a lecture at Johns Hopkins Medical School in Baltimore, describing his experimental work. The lecture was well attended and was greeted with enthusiasm. Excerpts of the lecture were published, and renowned medical journals requested that he submit his work for publication.

He described this trip in a letter to his mother:

"I visited the great Universities and the Hospitals of Baltimore, Philadelphia, and New York. They are infinitely superior to all that exist in Chicago or in France. From the material point of view, they are marvelous. I spent 24 delicious hours in Baltimore with Harvey Cushing at whose house I stayed. He has an old house whose back windows face the garden of Cardinal Gibbons. I spoke for an hour in frightful English in an Ampitheatre of

Johns Hopkins University and before the most eminent American scholars. I was happy to explain a few of my most bizarre ideas with great conviction. The next day I was in Philadelphia. The professors of the University there seemed equally superior to those in Chicago. Then in New York I visited the Rockefeller Institute for Medical Research and the Jewish Hospital of Mount Sinai which cost $25 million. It is a splendid palace. Because of the extraordinary things that I have written in medical journals, I am beginning to be known. This has permitted me to become friendly with several very remarkable men, in particular the Director of the Rockefeller Institute and the Chief Surgeon of Mt. Sinai Hospital, with whom I spent the whole day today."

Alexis' mother never read this letter. At the time of its writing she was acutely ill with uremia, and she died in a very few days. This was a severe blow to her son who had been extremely close to her. As a result he buried himself in his work and his experiments.

During the fall of 1905, a meeting of the Society for Clinical Surgery was held in Chicago. The meeting ended on Saturday noon. By prior arrangement Harvey Cushing, the rising surgeon from Johns Hopkins in Baltimore visited Carrel at the Hull Laboratory. Cushing was accompanied by Drs. Matas, Mumford and Finney. Dr. Matas of Tulane University was already one of the pioneer vascular surgeons of the world. Carrel performed an end to end anastomosis of the carotid artery of a dog for these distinguished surgeons.

Carrel received a letter from Guthrie in Columbia, Missouri, dated October 11, 1905:

"I hope your fears that someone else will steal our ideas may not materialize, but I think you are quite right in that we should publish at once in order to show the scope of our experiments. It is certain that it will be impossible to get it published in the October number of the *American Journal of Physiology* as Dr. Porter requires a manuscript six weeks in advance of publication. I think *Science* would be the earliest publication of any American journal and if you wish to send it there, the write up should be as short as possible. I regret that the work is so widely known at this time as our experiments are, I think, in the preliminary stages as yet—comparatively speaking of course. If such men as Cushing take it up now it means that we would be "beat out" in making human applications, as their facilities for such work are at present vastly superior to ours—you understand, I mean opportunities to get and operate suitable patients. Still I cannot believe that any one or set of surgeons can equal our results before they have worked much longer on the techniques than you and I together. I think it might be a good plan to keep the important details of the actual technique to ourselves for a time—not many of them will take the trouble to look up your first paper and besides I believe certain details are somewhat improved since then, are they not. A few blood clots would serve to cool their ardor."

The anxiety expressed in this letter may explain the brevity and lack of technical detail and the sparcity of illustrations in any of the papers written by Carrel and Guthrie from the Hull Laboratory.

Part of his responsibilities were teaching physiology to medical students. In an earlier letter to his mother he had written: "Our students continue to be very nice even though I talk too much and naturally in an incorrect fashion. One can't treat them like French students. In France, the more one puts on, the more important he is considered. Here it is better to be very simple and to chat with each one as if you had known him for twenty years. That's what I do. But at the same time, since I had to correct the copies of the exam that they had taken, I gave them lower grades than they deserved, 20, 60, 30, when they deserved at least 75. So when I talk, one can hear a fly in the classroom."

The greatest frustration that Carrel met in Chicago was the lack of financial support for his research. He was offered a clinical professorship but did not accept because he felt he would have to support his experimental work by developing a busy practice, something he did not want to do. He was offered a position at Johns Hopkins and another at the Rockefeller Institute. After careful consideration he accepted the latter. He wrote to his brother on May 16, 1906: "I received a letter from the Director of the Rockefeller Institute for Medical Research in New York telling me that I had been named to a post there by the last Assembly of Directors. It was the immediate result of my lecture at Johns Hopkins and of my visit to New York. The Rockefeller Institute is, though bigger and richer, similar to the Pasteur Institute in Paris. Besides, everything is absolutely new there because it has only been open for 15 days. I am going to accept immediately although it disgusts me to live in New York. New York is entirely built of high, high buildings and it seems that one is in prison, as in Lyon, for example . . . I will go there in September."

The building referred to above was the new Founders Building opened in 1906. The Rockefeller Institute itself was incorporated by John D. Rockefeller Sr. in 1901.

# CHAPTER IV

THE ROCKEFELLER INSTITUTE

T HE TURN OF THE CENTURY was the eve of the great American business magnates. Among the greatest of these in acumen and skill was John D. Rockefeller. He demonstrated the imagination and audacity to bring together the disjointed parts of the petroleum industry, the oil well producers, the refiners, and those who transported the oil, to form the Standard Oil Company which in the early 1900's dominated the oil markets of the world. Rockefeller had an unusual ability to select and guide men of talent, but all of these men freely acknowledged his superior creativity and sound judgment. Even his competitors sought his advice. As one of his associates said of him: "If he were placed in a group of any twenty of the greatest men of affairs today, he would be the most modest, retiring, and deferential man of them all, but before those giants had been with him long, the most self-confident, self-assertive of them would be coming to him in private for his counsel."

One of the major problems encountered by these extremely wealthy men, especially Rockefeller and Andrew Carnegie, was how to effectively dispose of the vast sums of money that they could not possibly spend upon themselves. A good bit of popular resentment had been created by such huge accumulations. This led to the development of philanthropic institutions and trusts which were to be used for public benefit. It became fashionable to give one's wealth away exemplifying Christian stewardship of the world's goods on behalf of the poor.

The Rockefeller Institute for Medical Research was incorporated in June 1901. It was first proposed to John D. Rockefeller Sr. by Frederick T. Gates, his executive director of philanthropy. Gates was a Baptist minister who first came to the attention of Rockefeller with his brilliant and forceful report to the American Baptist Education Society. In this report Gates pointed out the weakness of the denominational colleges in the midwest and the need for a University to provide them with intellectual leadership. In this report and in later correspondence, Rockefeller discovered the clear analytical thinking he needed after having listened to so many contending advocates, and he decided to make a gift of $600,000 to the University of Chicago in May 1889. Rockefeller hired Gates to manage his own philanthropy in 1891. Gates had to review and re-evaluate many projects, both institutional and private, which had developed from Rockefeller's gifts. Poorly planned and illogical programs and applications were eliminated. Gifts to churches, missions, and hospitals were centralized in reorganized church boards for more efficient utilization. Gates had the ideal characteristics for managing Rockefellers philanthropy: he could become enthusiastic for good causes and his creative imagination added to his effectiveness. This was balanced by a cold blooded business sense that allowed him to eliminate selfish or impractical projects. Gates allowed Rockefeller to enjoy the business of giving without the endless harassments to which he had been subjected.

For years, illness and treatment had been an interest to Gates, especially when, as pastor of a small congregation, he had much contact with patients and doctors. His experience led him to be very skeptical of physicians, their guess work methods of diagnosis and treatment, with no basis in science. This opinion was strengthened when he heard one of New York's most prominent physicians state that nine out of ten professional visits to the sick, for all the good they did, might just as well not have been made.

A young medical student, Elon O. Huntington, who had been a member of Gates congregation in Minneapolis, looked up his former minister when he came to New York to study at the College of Physicians and Surgeons. One day in 1897, three years after Gates joined Rockefeller's staff, he asked Huntington to suggest to him a medical book which a layman might understand, and from which he might gain a better insight into the effectiveness of medical treatment. Huntington, who was now a senior student, recommended Dr. William Osler's *Principles and Practice of Medicine*. Gates bought this book and, with a pocket medical dictionary, took it with him on vacation to the Catskills. Osler's textbook provided the best possible introduction to the field of medicine for a layman because of its readable style and humane outlook. It covered the entire field of disease and discussed the newest methods of treatment in a very objective fashion. Gates read the entire book—one thousand pages—from cover to cover and was fascinated. He felt that his skepticism about the state of medical practice was fully confirmed, but for the first time he began to realize the potential of scientific investigation in solving many of the mysteries of disease. According to Osler, even the most well-trained physician did not know specific cures for more than four or five diseases.

"In fact," wrote Gates, "I saw very clearly from the work of this able and honest man, that medicine had, with the few exceptions already mentioned, no cures, and that about all that medicine up to 1897 could do was to nurse the patients and alleviate in some degree the suffering."

"When I laid down this book, I had begun to realize how woefully neglected in all civilized countries and perhaps most of all in this country, had been the scientific study of medicine. I saw very clearly why this was true. In the first place, the instruments for investigation, the microscope, the science of chemistry, had not until recently been developed. Pasteur's germ theory of disease was very recent. Moreover, while other departments of science—astronomy, chemistry, physics, etc.—had been endowed very generously in colleges and universities throughout the whole civilized world, medicine, owing to the peculiar commercial organization of medical colleges, had rarely, if ever, been anywhere endowed, and research and instruction alike had been left to shift for itself, dependent altogether on such chance as the average practitioner might steal from his active practice."

In this statement Gates was exaggerating slightly. In Europe, medical research was receiving strong support in university laboratories and clinics, especially in Germany, and in a number of research institutes. Two of the latter he knew at least by name: The Koch Institute of Berlin and the Pasteur Institute of Paris. His allegations, however, were justified of the United States. He was quite right that "medicine could hardly hope to become a science until medical research should be endowed and qualified men could give themselves to the uninterrupted study and investigation, on ample salary, entirely independent of practice." Here was an opportunity, the greatest the world could afford, for Rockefeller to become a pioneer.

Gates and John D. Rockefeller Jr. persuaded the elder Rockefeller to establish a research institute, and a governing board of physicians and scientists was selected. Simon Flexner, professor of Pathology at the University of Pennsylvania, was selected as Director in June 1902. The Institute began in rented quarters and individual grants of money were awarded for specific projects. Consideration was given to establishing a University connection. Harvard and Columbia were interested but it was finally decided that a completely independent Institute was preferable, since this would avoid the burdensome routine of teaching and other academic responsibilities for the scientists.

A tract of land on Manhattan Island was purchased in late June, 1902. This property, known as the Schermerhorn tract, consisted of about thirteen acres of farm land on the East River between Sixty-Fourth and Sixty-Eighth Streets, the eastern half of which formed a rocky bluff about forty feet high overlooking the river and a wide stretch of Long Island. It was the last of the open tracts in a district once noted for its great suburban estates. When Rockefeller Jr. and the doctors inspected the old farm in June 1902, it presented almost the same appearance it had a century before. A few cows grazed on the gentle slope toward the western boundary, at Avenue A (now York Avenue); on the river side, Exterior Street (now Franklin D. Roosevelt Drive) had not been opened. The old Schermerhorn house, dating from the eighteenth century, stood perched on the very edge of the cliff, created by the cutting through of Sixty-fourth Street toward the river. Ground was broken for Founder's Building, the main hall, in July 1904. In April, 1905, Carrel paid it a visit, and by chance met its Director, Simon Flexner, who was inspecting the progress of the construction.

The original staff of the Rockefeller Institute was composed of Simon Flexner, Pathologist and Director, Higao Noguchi, Eugene L. Opie, J. H. Weeks, Pathologist, Samuel J. Meltzer,

Physiologist and Pharmacologist, and P. A. Levine, Biochemist. Carrel was appointed a fellow of the Institute in 1906, an associate member in 1910, and a full member in 1912.

Carrel moved to New York in 1906 and rented a small apartment in the Hotel Wellington at the corner of 7th Ave. and 56th Street, in the downtown area near Broadway, one of the noisiest districts in town. This did not seem to bother him, since the organization of his work at the Institute and his many walks served as a distraction. At the end of one year, he moved to be nearer his laboratory. He rented a small apartment near Sutton Place, nine blocks from the Institute.

Later he sought a place in the suburbs to escape traffic noise. He rented an apartment in the home of Mr. and Mrs. William Howe in White Plains, New York. Carrel became good friends with the Howe's. From White Plains the trip took 45 minutes by train to Grand Central Station, and another fifteen minutes on foot to reach the institute, but he found that the silence and solitude of the country were worth the daily two hour commuting. He did no entertaining in his apartment and had very little social life during this period.

Simon Flexner had great confidence in Carrel and provided ample laboratory space for him on the fifth floor of the main building. His unit was to be called the Experimental Surgery Department.

His first projects were a continuation of those on which he and Guthrie had worked in Chicago. He carried out five experiments in which he removed a segment of the abdominal aorta of a cat and replaced it with a segment of vein or artery from a dog. In each case the vascular heterograft had been removed from a dog several days or weeks prior to the experiment and preserved in a salt solution at about the freezing point. Several of these grafts thrombosed after three to ten days but at least one was still patent at seventy-seven days. Thus he showed for the first time that blood vessels could be preserved in cold saline and that arteries and veins could occasionally be grafted between species. Microscopic studies of the heterografts between species showed that after twenty days the muscular and elastic fibers which provide strength to the graft wall had degenerated almost completely, allowing a moderate to marked dilation of the graft, but this was compensated by a fibrous thickening of the outer (adventitial) or inner (intimal) layers of the graft so that rupture did not occur.

Between 1906 and 1910 he continued to work on the artery graft problem, and methods of preservation of grafts. A classic paper appeared in the *Journal of Experimental Medicine* in 1910 entitled "Latent Life of Arteries." In this paper he described experiments carried out over the course of several years, transplanting the carotid artery of one dog into the carotid artery of another, using different methods of preserving the grafted segment for periods of a few days to several months. He tried to discover if there was a difference in preservation techniques which killed the tissue, such as the use of heat, formalin and glycerin and those which preserved the graft in what he called "latent life." This latter condition was achieved by immersing the arteries in vaseline, then keeping them in cold storage at a temperature just above the freezing point. He found that grafts preserved for up to seventy days by this method had a 75 to 80 percent long term patency rate, as compared with a much lower patency rate for grafts which were treated by heat, by dehydration, or by preservation in glycerin or formalin.

It has since been shown that segments of artery that have been preserved by cold are also dead, but Carrel's conclusion has been confirmed that arterial preservation by cold is the least destructive method of preservation of the most important part of the wall of a vascular graft, the elastic fibers. His careful microscopic studies of the wall of the grafts after various periods of implantation revealed very clearly for the first time that arterial segments from other animals, whether of the same or a different species, degenerated slowly or rapidly depending on the method of preservation, and were replaced by fibrous tissue from the host. This resulted in a scar tissue tube that could still carry arterial blood at arterial pressure without forming a dilation or aneurysm. The strength-giving elastic membrane was much better preserved in homografted arteries between animals of the same species than with grafts between different species.

In another experiment, begun in Chicago and completed in

New York, he used an oval shaped segment of peritoneal lining to patch surgically created openings in the abdominal aorta. To the naked eye these patches of endothelial tissue produced a normal aortic wall but, again, under the microscope he discovered that the original peritoneal tissue had been completely replaced by connective tissue.

All these experiments showed for the first time that any kind of tissue except autologous artery (an artery from the same animal) served only as a scaffolding for the development of a connective tissue tube (scar), but that this tube could function as an arterial conduit for at least eighteen to twenty four months. Clinical experiences in the 1950's and 1960's have borne out these observations in humans.

At about this time, 1908 to 1910, Samuel J. Meltzer, head of the laboratory of physiology and pharmacology at the Rockefeller Institute, with his young assistant (and son-in-law), John Auer, began working on the physiological action of magnesium and other salts. Magnesium sulfate, they found, when injected subcutaneously in suitable doses, produces unconsciousness and complete muscular relaxation, from which the animal recovers rapidly if given an injection of calcium chloride. Meltzer hoped that magnesium sulfate could be used as a surgical anesthetic. Although this proved impractical he had the satisfaction of seeing his discovery widely used to diminish muscular spasm in desperate cases of tetanus, eclampsia, and other serious conditions.

Because the chief danger of the use of magnesium in surgery was the risk of inhibiting the respiratory center of the brain, Meltzer and Auer studied the currently available methods of artificial respiration. They hit upon the idea of keeping the lungs inflated by a stream of air blown through a tube inserted into the windpipe by way of the mouth or nasal passage. If a steady flow of air was delivered into the trachea through a small loosely fitting tube positioned so that the end lay just proximal to the carina, the division of the trachea into its two major bronchi, the blood could be aerated without any respiratory movements of the chest. By including ether or some other anesthetic vapor in the air stream, an animal or human patient could readily be kept under surgical anesthesia. This invention was immediately taken over by the surgeons to solve some of their problems. In the first place, it solved a great difficulty in operations about the face and throat, by getting the anesthetist and his ether mask out of the surgeon's way. Better still, it was the simplest practical method for keeping the lungs inflated after the chest was opened. The only means thoracic surgeons had formerly had to avoid collapse of the lung upon opening the chest and losing the natural vacuum that keeps lungs expanded, was to place the patient and surgical team in a cumbersome low pressure chamber, filled with pipes and gauges as in a submarine. Henceforth they could work in an ordinary operating room, keeping the lungs inflated by air under suitable pressure through a Meltzer-Auer tube. Alexis Carrel saw the potential at once and began to use the method in experimental thoracic surgery, and within a few years it was adopted by hospitals everywhere. Thus Meltzer's work facilitated the development of modern chest and heart surgery by allowing the lungs to be ventilated with the thoracic cavity open.

In 1909 Carrel began to use endotracheal anesthesia as it was taught to him by Meltzer. He stated in a paper published in the *Journal of the American Medical Association* in January, 1910, "I immediately tried it in a few simple experiments, such as the resection of a pulmonary lobe, the extirpation of a segment of the middle part of the esophagus, followed by a circular suture, the dissection of the mediastinum by opening the two pleurae and the pericardium, and resection of a small part of the superior vena cava and its replacement by a piece of jugular vein. The animals recovered completely, with the exception of one that died of pleurisy a few days after operation." He went on to describe some experiments on the thoracid aorta. He divided and quickly resutured the descending aorta, keeping it occluded for only six and one half minutes. In another experiment he grafted a segment of a large vena cava preserved in cold storage into the descending aorta after removing a corresponding segment. The circulation was interrupted for seventeen minutes. The animal awoke with paralysis of the hind limbs due to ischemia of the spinal cord. This was new information, that paraplegia could be produced by prolonged occlusion of the descending thoracic aorta. Carrel learned to prevent this by inserting a paraffined tube into the aortic lumen and allowing blood to flow through this tube while a graft was sutured into the aorta. The tube could be quickly removed through a small slit in the aorta below the graft. Carrel found that he could work on the aorta for much longer periods, twenty-five or thirty minutes at least, without the development of hind limb paralysis.

Another method he explored in his efforts to prevent spinal cord ischemia while resecting portions of the descending thoracic aorta was "lateral diversion." This consisted of establishing a communication between the left ventricle of the heart and the descending aorta. A paraffined rubber tube was inserted into the apex of the left ventricle and fastened; the other end was inserted into the descending thoracic aorta. This would allow work on the more proximal part of the descending aorta while the more distal part was being supplied directly from the ventricle.

Perhaps the most amazing experiments that Carrel conducted in 1909 to 1910 were those he attempted on the heart itself. The following is a quote from a paper he gave before the august American Surgical Association, May 10, 1910:

"I attempted to find out some method for the treatment of valvular diseases and localized sclerosis of the coronarian arteries. Theoretically, many operations can be performed on the heart, incision and dilation of stenosed valves, cuneiform resection and stenosis of the upper part of the ventricle in case of mitral insufficiency, curretage (scraping) of endocardiac vegetations, grafting of new vessels on the auricles and ventricles, collateral circulation between two cavities of the heart, direct coronarian anastamosis, etc. Plastic operations on the heart are not very much more difficult than on any other part of the body. But to perform the operations without disturbing in an irreparable manner the functions of the nervous system and of the heart itself is a very complicated problem . . .

The cardiac operations can be artificially divided into three classes: operations which do not require the hemotasis of the heart (interruption of blood returning to the heart), operations which require the hemostasis for a very short time, and operations which require hemostasis for a longer time and the stopping of the heart.

1. Several operations can be performed without the help of the temporary hemostasis, such as digital explorations of the ventricles or the auricles, dilation of the mitral valve, dissection and preparation of a coronarian vessel for anastomosis, incomplete ventriculectomy and suture, etc. I tried to develop an operation for mitral insufficiency which could be performed without opening the heart. It consists of producing a slight stenosis of the upper part of the left ventricle. It can be obtained by a partial cuneiform resection of the wall of the ventricle just below the coronary artery. A dog which has undergone this partial ventriculectomy two months ago is still alive and in good health.

2. In the operations of the second class, the cavities of the heart are open for about one minute, during which time it becomes possible to insert and fix a tube or vessel into the ventricular or auricular cavities, to open largely and suture the ventricular wall. It would also be feasible to cut a mitral or tricuspidian valve, or to perform curretage of endocardiac vegetations. I tried to determine what are the best conditions under which this type of operation must be performed. The hemostasis can be secured by the clamping of the venae cavae as advocated by Sauerbruch. But it is simpler to clamp with a soft jawed forceps the entire pedicle of the heart. As the interruption of the circulation does not last more than one or two minutes, it causes no cerebral complications. The main danger is the occurrence of fibrillary contractions, which render almost impossible the re-establishment of normal pulsations. I performed clamping of the heart eight times, with or without cardiotomy, for from one to five minutes. One dog died of respiratory complications, another of fibrillary contractions.

3. To the third class belong the operations requiring the interruption of the circulation for a longer time. They would consist of more complicated plastic operations on the cardiac wall, and of the operations on the coronarian arteries. In certain cases of angina pectoris, when the mouth of the coronary arteries is calcified, it would be useful to establish a complementary circulation for the lower part of the arteries. I attempted to perform an indirect anastamosis between the descending aorta and the left coronary artery. It was, for many reasons, a difficult opera-

tion. On account of the continuous motion of the heart, it was not easy to dissect and suture the artery. In one case I implanted one end of a long carotid artery, preserved in cold storage, on the descending aorta. The other end was passed through the pericardium and anastamosed to the peripheral end of the coronary near the pulmonary artery. Unfortunately the operation was too slow. Three minutes after the interruption of the circulation, fibrillary contraction appeared, but the anastamosis took five minutes. By massage of the heart the dog was kept alive but he died two hours later."

In these experiments Carrel anticipated much of modern heart surgery such as mitral valvulotomy, mitral annuloplasty, excision of ventricular aneurysms, and even direct grafting procedures for obstructive coronary artery disease. These techniques were not to see clinical utilization until the late 1940's and early 1950's, and direct coronary artery surgery did not become established until the late 1960's.

In 1909, the premature infant son of a New York doctor developed on the third day of his life the dangerous disease melena neonatorium, in which blood oozes from the surface of the entire gastrointestinal tract. There were at that time two cases on record of babies with this disease who had been saved by blood transfusion. This baby was considered too small for the usual technique of transfusion, connecting the radial artery of the donor to the vein of the recipient with a small tube or cannula. The father, who had seen Carrel work on animals, appealed to him for help. After careful consideration of the various possibilities, Carrel suggested suturing the father's radial artery to the baby's popliteal vein, behind the knee. An end-to-end anastomosis between these two vessels was accomplished after several attempts by Carrel. One of the surgeons assisting described the baby's vein as being the size of a matchstick and the texture of wet cigarette paper. When the anastomosis was finally completed and the clamps removed, blood flowed rapidly from father to child and within minutes the pale child turned a normal pink. The child recovered completely. Mr. Rockefeller Sr. heard about the dramatic operation and was so deeply impressed that he included the tale in his book, *Random Reminiscences of Men and Events.*

Of all the exciting research going on at the Rockefeller Institute from 1906 to the beginning of the First World War, none created more public interest than Carrel's work with cultures of living tissue. Scientists were excited about the technique as a new way of studying life processes. Newspaper accounts discussed tissue culture as evidence of immortality, describing and showing photographs of living cells multiplying and growing in glass tubes, long after the death of the animal from which the cells were taken.

Carrel's reason for attempting to grow tissues outside the body was to allow him to study the mechanism by which wounds heal, an interest of his for some years. He wanted to learn how cells of the skin, connective tissue, blood vessels and nerves could cross the gap between the edges of a wound and reorganize themselves to heal the injuries caused by disease, trauma or surgery. He hoped by removing cells from the body to discover how much of this reparative process was carried on by the cells themselves and what part was due to the organizing ability of the body. His ultimate aim was to develop ways of speeding the healing of wounds. His work in artery grafting and organ transplantation had given him hope that it might be possible to keep human organs and tissues alive in storage and even to grow new organs for replacement parts.

Carrel first learned about tissue culture when he heard a Harvey lecture in New York in March 1908. Ross G. Harrison of Yale, in this address, described for the first time success in growing living cells outside the body. The method was developed to study the mechanism by which nerve fibers develop in an embryo to connect its various parts. Some embryologists thought that fibers grew out of individual nerve cells in the brain, spinal cord or outlying ganglion, even to great lengths. Others thought that nerve fibers were formed from short lengths produced by local cells and then connected end to end. Harrison cut out a section of the spinal cord of a chick embryo and placed it in a clear drop of clotted lymph on a hollowed out glass microscope slide. Under the microscope he was able to watch the nerve fiber grow, unobscured by other tissues. This proved the first of the two theories of nerve cell development, as Harrison showed serial photographs of nerve fibers sprouting from nerve cells and growing longer daily as far as the lymph allowed them to spread.

Intrigued by the possibilities he could foresee in this technique, Carrel asked permission to visit Yale and learn Harrison's techniques so that he could modify it for wound healing research. Flexner suggested, however, that he send young Montrose T. Burrows, who had begun work as Carrel's assistant in 1909 directly out of medical school. Burrows spent several months with Harrison in the spring of 1910 and improved upon the tissue culture medium of clotted lymph by substituting blood plasma( the fluid part of blood freed of its white and red cells). When plasma clots, it forms a mesh, a stroma upon which cells can grow, and has the advantage of being easier to obtain than lymph.

Burrows experimented with embryonic nerve, skin and heart tissue on his improved culture medium and stumbled on a completely unexpected discovery. The cultured embryonic heart muscle, cut off from all nervous control, continued to contract or "beat," solving a long debated question as to whether the heart muscle contracted due to external nerve stimulation or to intrinsic (myogenic) control.

When Burrows returned to the Rockefeller Institute, he and Carrel attempted to grow malignant (cancer) cells on tissue culture. They were successful in growing the Rous fowl sarcoma— even to a second generation. Attempts were made to culture tissues of adult dogs and cats. They chose quite complicated tissues, such as thyroid and kidney, and the cells that grew out seemed to arrange themselves in a way to suggest the tissues from which they came. Carrel, in this case, let his excitement cloud his scientific judgment, and published a report in October 1910 that suggested that he had grown several kinds of highly organized adult tissues. This paper was soundly criticized. In November 1910 he gave a similar paper before the Societe de Biologie of Paris. Before this distinguished forum he described primary, secondary and tertiary cultures of the thyroid glands. He was immediately attacked for drawing erroneous conclusions by a famous biologist, A. Jolly, who wrote in the Society's Compte Rendus that there was no thyroid epithelium in the third generation culture, or even in the second. What had actually grown out was largely, perhaps entirely, connective tissue cells. What appeared to be thyroid cells in the primary cultures (from what was learned later) were in these early crude, insufficiently nourished cultures, probably old cells already existing in the tissue before it was cultured.

Carrel tried to overwhelm his critics by showmanship. He determined to keep one of the embryonic heart cultures alive through as many generations as possible, until every doubter was convinced. The now famous heart culture dating from January 12, 1912, was first reported in April when it was 85 days old and had passed thirty generations. The care of this culture was turned over to Albert H. Ebeling, then a technician, in June of 1912. Little did he know that this chore would last 34 years. Not only was this heart culture a source of publicity in the popular press, but it became the standard tissue in Carrel's lab against which to test changes in the culture media and other environmental factors.

Carrel discovered how to increase greatly the growth of cells in tissue cultures. In 1909 to 1910, he had demonstrated that poultices of crushed animal tissues seemed to speed up the healing of experimental skin wounds. This led him to add extracts of chick embryo to his plasma medium and he found that it produced increased growth of the cells. Even today, tissue culture workers put embryo extract in their media without being sure how it functions to increase cell growth.

In May 1914, the heart culture was over three years old, had been through 358 generations and because of improved techniques was growing much faster than earlier. If all the accumulated cells had been kept, they would have far exceeded the size of the original embryo. The culture was now so strong and vigorous it had to be subcultured only once a week. Frequently reported in the popular press, the "chicken heart culture" had become known all over the world—in spite of the fact that the heart muscle cells it originally contained had long since died out, leaving only connective tissue cells (fibroblasts). Still overseeing the care of the heart culture, Ebeling took his MD degree, then became a member of the scientific staff of the Rockefeller Institute. He took the culture with him when he left the Institute to direct tissue culture work at the Lederle Laboratories where it was used to test the toxicity of germicides until April 1946 when it was discontinued two years after Carrel's death and 34 years after it was first explanted from the embryonic chick heart. This experiment did prove Jolly wrong when he doubted Carrel's right to call his preparation a "culture," but Jolly was correct in his criticism that the early tissue cultures did not contain epithelial gland cells. Ebeling and Albert Fischer were finally able to culture epithelial cells in 1922; earlier cultures contained only connective tissue cells.

The contribution of Carrel and his associates to the field of tissue culture was the development of techniques of cultivating tissues of warm blooded animals. Carrel had two talents which helped him make this contribution. The first was his understanding of aseptic technique, since contaminating bacteria could completely destroy a culture. His second great talent, manual dexterity which he developed through his experience with blood vessel surgery was very useful in being able to cut thin enough slices of tissue for culturing. This is now done by mechanical slicers. Later investigators with greater powers of scientific analysis were to use the tissue culture method Carrel had placed in their hands to answer many important questions of biology and chemistry. It was to find many applications in the field of medical science—the study of cell structure and cell life, the understanding of cancer, the knowledge of viruses and the preparation of vaccines.

In the cancer field, Carrel and his associates were able to show that tumor cells cultivated outside the organism retain their malignancy indefinitely; that cultures of malignant cells are often indistinguishable from normal cells, that the rate of proliferation of normal and malignant cells growing in cultures is remarkably similar; and that differences in food requirements of normal and malignant cells, growing in cultures in natural media, are actually no greater than those existing between various types of normal cells. Carrel, in 1932, suggested that the factor responsible for malignancy might consist of a virus coming from without, one manufactured by the cells themselves, a ferment multiplying at the surface of the cells, or a simple mutation. Years later, all of these various possibilities are still being investigated.

Carrel found immense satisfaction in the American temperament and way of life. He admired the seriousness, the punctuality, the simplicity in the style of those around him. He shaved his beard, and adopted many American habits, but he was too deeply imprinted by his provincial French to abandon a certain air that was typically Carrel. He maintained his own distinct habits and personality and was for many years known as "the Frenchman of the Rockefeller Institute." He had become quite bald with a crown of hair, always closely shaven, covered with a white surgical cap that he wore pulled far down nearly to his eyes and from which he was hardly ever separated. His usual attire at the Institute was this white cap, white trousers, and a short white jacket adjusted in the middle by a brown leather belt.

Although he won almost fanatical devotion from some of his immediate helpers, Carrel held himself aloof from the general life of the Institute. Working largely by himself, he rarely consulted colleagues. His laboratory rooms, necessarily guarded against bacterial contamination, acquired the aura of a sanctuary where masked acolytes clad in black gowns and caps performed the aseptic mysteries of experimental surgery and tissue culture. Early in his career Carrel adopted black surgical gowns and drapes for his operating table to cut down glare and give better visibility to the tissues upon which he performed his extremely delicate operations. People from other laboratories, fearing to carry infectious germs into the laboratory, did not drop in for casual visits and never learned what was going on, except when specially invited. Even at the lunch table, Carrel did not fully unbend, often entering after the others were seated, wearing his surgeon's cap as a badge (thought some of his colleagues) of hieratic distinction. Many rumors about cloistral seclusiveness at the Institute can be traced to the impact of his unique personality.

Visitors found it necessary to visit him at his laboratory at the Institute; he seldom received anyone elsewhere. As his reputation grew it was occasionally necessary for him to entertain notable people with more ceremony. He would have dinner at his club, or if there were women, in the restaurant of one of the large hotels. Most of those whom he favored with an invitation to dine, after the traditional tour of his laboratory or more rarely after attendance at an experiment, had to be content with the modest menu served to the staff in the large dining room of the Institute.

At first he was proud of his growing renown, pleased above all to show his former Lyonnaise colleagues and friends and relations in France what he was doing. Soon, however, he tired of this increasing flood of visitors. His secretary for thirty years, Miss K. Crutcher, had to become the guardian of his privacy following Carrel's instructions in this regard. She made appointments and tactfully encouraged the more insistent visitors to be a little more patient. Nevertheless there was increasing publicity, and the increasing demand for interviews irritated Carrel, and he frequently lost his temper when he felt this was interfering with his work. René Leriche, whom Carrel particularly liked and respected, recounted his own difficulties when he visited Carrel by invitation. The first morning he was turned away, and was quite surprised. The same thing occurred the second morning. The third morning when rebuffed again, he became quite angry, as his time was limited, and insisted upon admission. Carrel was upset at this inadvertant rudeness to his friend, and made up for it by throwing open the doors of his laboratory, and by reserving long periods of time for conversation. Carrel also opened other doors for Leriche to medical centers in the United States. He telephoned surgical friends in Chicago, the Mayo Clinic, and Johns Hopkins to introduce his compatriot. A recommendation from Carrel had become of great importance in the American medical world.

A witness of his first four or five years in New York said of him, "He lived in a small apartment next to mine where he did little other than sleep. He spent his days, and often his evenings, in his laboratory even taking his meals there." During these years the passion with which he threw himself into his work was extreme. Then more and more he began to relax, and became more a master rather than a slave of his time. In general, he arrived at his laboratory before eight o'clock, checked on the conditions of his animals, and on the experiment planned for that day. Then he discussed in detail the plans for the day with his collaborators.

Toward the middle of the morning he donned his black surgical gown, and his surgical magnifying glasses required by the minuteness of his experiments. After an hour or so, when he had completed the most arduous part of the operation, or experimented with some new procedure, he turned the experiment over to his most qualified assistant. Before lunch he reserved a few minutes for appointments and interviews. The afternoons were usually spent writing, editing notes, making further observations on current experiments, or planning future work with his collaborators. There were periodic meetings of the scientific staff of the Institute which he attended, presenting his own work and learning of the work of his colleagues. The day was usually over at five o'clock but Carrel often remained longer because he judged his presence useful to the experiments in progress. At certain periods, when, for example, he began the culture of tissues or later, the artificial heart, he spent the entire night working in his laboratory.

# CHAPTER V

THE NOBEL PRIZE

After Carrel had been in New York for two years, he felt the desire to return to France, to resume old acquaintances, to see relatives and to take care of business matters which had been neglected since his mother's death. An annual vacation was allowed at the Rockefeller Institute; this allowed Carrel to cross the Atlantic each June, and to return in early September. In this way he avoided the stifling heat of Manhattan summers. He usually spent the first two weeks of June in Paris visiting the large surgical clinics where he had become well known because of his numerous scientific publications. July he usually passed at "La Batie" near Saint-Martin-en-Haut. This beautiful chateau that his mother had bought in 1901, two years before his departure to America, remained in his family until 1942. (At that time La Batie was sold without Carrel being able to acquire it due to insufficient funds). He loved this beautiful retreat, the landscape of his youth, the old servants he knew so well, the acquaintances he met on a walk. He enjoyed the family life with his brother and sister, his brother-in-law, Guigou, and their children. In addition to the companionship he enjoyed the isolation, which he found on long walks he took in the surrounding countryside. Carrel never missed spending at least a part of each summer at "La Batie" even after 1922 when he acquired an estate on the island of St. Gildas in Brittany. Old photographs show him dressed in a bulky sweater, an English cap, golf culottes and high tennis shoes. He seldom visited nearby Lyon, but he did maintain contact with his former fellow workers who had become, for the most part, departmental directors and administrators.

To those who had known him in Lyon, Carrel was the prodigal child of whom everyone was proud, but whose indiscretions no one had forgotten. Carrel, on the other hand could still see in his homeland the imperfections that he had repudiated before. He was proud of his membership in the famous Rockefeller Institute. He was convinced of the superiority of his working conditions, and he often made known this sentiment. Certain individuals were irritated by this condescending attitude. They nicknamed him "the American." Throughout his life this antagonism remained between Carrel and his French colleagues, especially those in Lyon.

Each year in August Carrel made his annual pilgrimage to Lourdes. He had never forgotten the miraculous cure he had witnessed years before, but even more than the memory, his curiosity persuaded him to return, to observe, and to discuss other cases with Dr. Boissarie, chief of the office of medicine. In 1910 Carrel observed an eighteen month old child, born blind, miraculously recover its sight, while being held in the arms of a nurse. That same evening when the crowd had dispersed, Carrel wandered throughout the area, absorbed in thought. A striking woman dressed in mourning was sitting quietly on one of the benches. Recognizing her, he approached and asked, "Aren't you the nurse who brought that little blind child here and observed that miracle this afternoon?" "Yes, it was I," she replied. Carrel questioned her for a long time. They met again the following day, and corresponded frequently over the next two years.

Madame de la Meyrie, 35 years old, was born Anne-Marie Laure Gourlez de la Motte. She married Monsieur de la Mayrie and later had a son. Her husband died in 1909, leaving her a widow. Deeply religious, she devoted herself to charity and to nursing. Each summer she participated in the pilgrimage from Brittany to Lourdes. Carrel, who was then almost forty, was for the first time in his life attracted to a woman. Her family, Gourlez de la Motte, belonged to the aristocracy. Carrel was a bourgeois Lyonnaise of common lineage, but his ancestors had occupied honorable positions in the third estate. Madame was tall, beautiful, elegant; she was an ardent adventuress, and had a taste for risk. She was interested in sports, sold horses and drove an automobile. She was straightforward and outspoken. In Paris she had taken courses in Red Cross, and worked on the surgical service of Dr. Tuffier, a friend of Carrel's. He found her charming. They shared many common interests, such as beauty, religion, the miracles of Lourdes, tradition, progress, etc.

During the summer of 1912, Madame de la Meyrie came to Lyon to spend a few days with some of her personal friends. Carrel introduced her to his family, and to some of his more intimate friends. They talked of marriage, but Madame de la Meyrie was very much attached to her family and to her province. She had an independent nature, and with her interests in sports and the care of her five year old son, she felt reluctant to leave for the United States. There she would have to change completely her method of living, share a laborious vocation, and become a slave to Carrel's career. She asked to postpone making a final decision. They separated on September 7, Carrel sailing for New York while she returned to her nursing responsibilities.

Carrel occasionally took short vacations in the fall and spring when the press of work produced exhaustion, and when he felt the need for solitude. Maine and Vermont were his favorite spots.

In 1908, when Carrel was returning by ship from France he became acquainted with Frederic R. Coudert, a New York lawyer of French descent whose specialty was international law and who was highly esteemed in America. A friendship began which lasted 35 years. A strong bond developed between these two men as they found they shared common opinions of France, Europe, America and many other things. Upon arriving in New York, Coudert invited Carrel to dine at his club. That dinner included Samuel Butler, Professor of Philosophy at Columbia University, whom Carrel immediately liked. This affair became a weekly occasion with a select attendance. Carrel attended regularly when he was in town.

Frederic Coudert was much more sociable and outgoing than Carrel and deplored the monastic existence led by the scientist. He tried to distract him, invited Carrel to spend weekends at his property at Oyster Bay Long Island, but only succeeded in stimulating Carrel's interest in horseback riding. Alexis had done a little riding in Lyon in his adolescence. He joined the Piping Rock Sports Club, rented and finally bought a pony that he rode on Sundays.

One morning in October 1912, in glancing at a New York morning paper, Carrel noticed his name in the headlines. He read the paragraph and learned that the Caroline Institute of Stockholm had just awarded him the Nobel Prize for Physiology and Medicine. At the Rockefeller Institute, a cable was waiting officially notifying him of the award. He was surprised, even though he knew Dr. Carl Beck, Professor of Surgery at the University of Illinois (with whom he had worked briefly in Chicago) had nominated him in 1909. Dr. Beck, who was an American representative of the Nobel Prize committee wrote Carrel telling him of his recommendation at that time.

Telegrams of congratulations poured in. Flexner called to express his great satisfaction, while on the first floor of the Institute, the administrator of the building could hardly contain the group of reporters and photographers. Though he was still a citizen of France (and always remained one), he was the first scientist in America to be awarded this prize. He was also the youngest Nobel laureate, being just eight months short of his fortieth birthday. President William Howard Taft sent a congratulatory message, and later spoke at a ceremony in his honor, celebrating the event.

"The names of Harvey, Pasteur, Walter Reed, Koch, are great names which share the progress toward a superior knowledge of the human and of medicine, and from now on, Dr. Carrel will take his place among them," said the President on this occasion.

Carrel was not happy when he learned that it was necessary for him to go personally to Stockholm to receive the prize and the $40,000 that was awarded with it. At first he refused to go and much persuasion was required to convince him that such a refusal would be insolent and discourteous. In December he left for Sweden alone, not planning to stop en route. He wrote a letter from the ship saying, "It is a very beautiful boat. I have not been able to work since I was recognized by the Germans, Swedes, and Belgians aboard from my photographs in the American newspapers. My dream to live as a hermit for eight days has flown away to my great regret. I hope to be on my way back to New York soon. I'm in a hurry to have this all over."

According to the statutes of the Nobel Foundation, the annual distribution of prizes was scheduled for the 10th of December, the anniversary of the death of the great benefactor. The solemn meeting took place at six in the evening in the large room of the

Royal Academy of Music, adorned with a bust of Alfred Nobel, and richly decorated with emblems and flowers. The King of Sweden graciously presented each prize to its winner. The court consisted of Prince William, Prince Charles, and the Princess Ingeborg and their following. Also present were members of the diplomatic corps, and of the Swedish Ricksdag, and the Mayor of Stockholm. There were prominent men of business, and civil and military leaders on hand, as well as Dr. Manuel Nobel representing the family.

Before the distribution of each prize took place, there was a speech by the President of the Committee. The following is an abstract of the speech for Carrel by Professor J. Ackerman: "To the great intelligence you have received from your mother country, France, to whom humanity owes so many great things, is united the energy and resolve of your adopted country. Your miraculous operations are the evident result of this happy collaboration. Your animal experiments have multiplied the means of cure of wounds and diseases which strike us all and have created great renown for the name of Carrel in the domain of medic'ne. The new pathways you have opened of replacing damaged or noxious tissue with healthy and living tissue are so remarkable and the results obtained so marvelous that the Carolina Institute believes it is acting in perfect conformity with the wish of the great donor in conveying to you, Dr. Carrel, the greatest distinction in medicine, the Nobel Prize."

That evening at seven o'clock during the Nobel Banquet and the festivities that followed a speech was given by Professor Soderbaum: "Dr. Carrel of all our foreign guests, you have come the furthest. You have crossed the ocean to come to us, but deep down, the distance is not important. A man who like you has done so much for humanity and in particular for suffering humanity has the right to be any place in the whole universe. In whatever part of the world he takes himself and to whatever part of the world he comes, he has the right to be regarded as a fellow citizen, a benefactor, a friend."

Carrel sailed almost immediately for New York to resume his work.

In France, as well as elsewhere, the award of the Nobel Prize to Alexis Carrel was much discussed. The government recognized the importance of the award being given to a French citizen and made him a Knight of the Legion of Honor on February 17, 1913. During the summer vacation of 1913, he was honored by his former colleagues of Lyon by being asked to give a lecture in the great amphitheater of the old Faculty of Medicine. Almost two hundred people attended. Professor Courmont presided, and introduced Carrel as the scientist who had left Lyon ten years before as an unknown, and now returned with renown. The lecture was a great success and was followed by the applause of the university authorities, colleagues, and students. A large reception and dinner followed sponsored by former friends and teachers.

In spite of these honors, Carrel remained bitterly critical of French "decadence and bureaucracy." In a letter he stated, "The French renaissance about which we talk in New York is already far gone. Everywhere there are evident signs of a profound decadence, littleness, stinginess, cowardliness of those in important situations. French politicians are becoming more and more distasteful. The government isn't even capable of preventing sabotage of the railroads."

At a large dinner in Paris at the home of the philosopher, Henri Bergson, the guests were discussing the epidemics that were decimating the French army in Morocco. Crudel asked "But how can we let the soldiers die without remedy?" Metchinikoff responded: "The vaccines are inefficient." Coudert turned to Carrel and asked, "What does Dr. Carrel think about this?"

"They are too ignorant in France to plan for the future," he replied from the end of the table. These words fell in a dismayed silence.

Alexis and Anne Marie de la Meyrie officially became engaged during the summer of 1913. Together the couple visited relatives and friends in Paris at the end of August and the wedding was planned for December. An old photograph shows Carrel with his brother and sister and fiancée having dinner together at a restaurant on the island in the Bois de Boulogne. Anne wore a long dress belted at the waist and a hat with a wide brim, while Alexis wore a tuxedo, and held his gloves in his hand.

On September 3, 1913, Carrel sailed for New York but re-

Figure 9. Alexis Carrel and Anne Marie de la Meyrie just before their marriage in Paris in 1913.

turned to Paris in mid December where he and Anne were married on December 26. A civil ceremony took place in the morning, followed by a religious ceremony in the evening at the Church of Saint Pierre du Gros. That same evening a train took the couple to Cherbourg, where they boarded the boat for New York and sailed the following day.

Arriving in New York, they rented a home outside of town in Garden City and acquired an automobile. Carrel's friends derived much humor from his misadventures as a chauffeur. He was so distracted and absent minded that he would often take one way roads going the wrong way, and would sometimes inadvertantly drive on the sidewalks. He was frequently stopped by the police who soon came to know his eccentricities. When he finally realized he was not going to improve, he turned the driving over to his wife. If friends teased him about his driving, Carrel did not reply but wrinkled his nose with a wry smile. Later they moved into Manhattan and sold the car.

Carrel's marriage did not diminish the activity in his department at the Rockefeller Institute. Madame Carrel, who had studied nursing and had received a diploma from the French Red Cross, became an important part of the experimental surgical team. Work was then just beginning on corneal grafts, the very delicate task of transplanting the transparent membrane in front of the eye of one animal to another. Carrel received an invitation in the spring of 1914 to come to Germany to give a series of scientific lectures but he responded with a polite refusal since he did not wish to take the time away from his work.

In mid June, 1914, the Carrels sailed for France on their annual vacation, little realizing that it would be several years before their return. Upon arriving in France they received a cable informing them that Carrel's uncle was desperately ill in Lyon. They proceeded there immediately, arriving too late to see him alive. After a few days they left for the Chateau de Moulines in the province of Anjou which belonged to the family of Anne Carrel, who was now expecting a child.

# CHAPTER VI

THE FIRST WORLD WAR

J ULY OF 1914 was a restful, happy month for the Carrels at the chateau in Anjou. They were for the most part unaffected by the echo of Sarajevo and the clouds of war that were gathering over Europe.

One beautiful afternoon in late July Madame Carrel suffered a painful bee sting which was followed by a violent anaphylactic reaction with respiratory difficulty and fever. She remained ill for several weeks and the toxic reaction resulted in the death of her unborn child. Several more weeks passed before she recovered completely.

In the midst of his wife's illness, on August 1st, Carrel, as a French citizen, received his mobilization orders and instructions to report immediately to Lyon. War broke out in mid August. Carrel was stationed in the center of the marshalling yard in Lyon. Train loads of wounded began to arrive from the combat area; he examined them to decide if they should be transported further from the fighting or attended there. Until the battle of the Marne the wounded arrived in relatively satisfactory condition. The wounding projectiles were primarily bullets, the stagnant warfare of the trenches did not yet exist, and serious infections had not yet made their appearance. At first, Carrel, who was completely inexperienced in war surgery, was proud of the quality of the French health service, but soon afterwards the first cases of gas gangrene arrived; these serious cases increased after October. This terrible infection continued to increase; the French surgeons were completely unprepared. Carrel was transferred to the old Hotel Dieu in Lyon, where he was assigned to work with his friend Professor Leon Berard. Here, in a decrepit ward he began a systematic study of these extremely serious war wound infections.

The healing of wounds was not a new interest to Carrel, although admittedly it had been a minor one in the past. From his laboratory at the Rockefeller Institute, Carrel had published a paper in the *Journal of the American Medical Association* in 1910 entitled "The Treatment of Wounds, A First Article." He carefully excised rectangular segments of the dog skin, then covered the wound with aseptic dressings. He studied the different stages of the natural process of healing, using only black dogs who always healed with a white scar, thus allowing him to measure accurately at any time the original edges of the wound. Every clean wound went through predictable stages of healing, he found.

With the appearance of badly infected war wounds, his interest in wound healing was rekindled. For some reason gas gangrene had not been particularly prevalent in previous wars. Perhaps the more mutilating shrapnel and higher velocity weapons caused more devitalization of tissues than in previous conflicts. Serious infections were more frequent when wounding occurred in freshly tilled fields, especially if fertilized by animal dung which contained the clostridium of gas gangrene and the spores of tetanus. Wounds became more seriously infected in cold wet weather, and when a raging battle prevented rapid collecting and transporting of wounded. Soldiers injured by shells, trench mortars, grenades, mines, etc., suffered much destruction and mangling of tissues. These complicated wounds contained in their recesses not only projectiles, but dirt, clothing, pebbles, and all sorts of foreign bodies. The standard method of treatment of such wounds at the beginning of the war was a brief irrigation, removal of all foreign material possible, final irrigation with an antiseptic solution, and partial closure with adequate drainage.

Carrel soon realized that these methods of treatment were inadequate and he began to experiment with various antiseptic agents, such as boric acid solution, to irrigate the wound. He tried to persuade the local authorities to provide him a laboratory and a chemist so that he might conduct organized experiments in the prevention of wound infection, but he met with no success.

One day in November, 1914, James Hazen Hyde, a wealthy and influential American living in Paris, was motoring across France with his wife on the way to the coast. He had met Carrel several years before and they had become firm friends. Hyde accidentally encountered Carrel on a sidewalk in Lyon, and was immediately disturbed by the distressed look on Carrel's face. Hyde asked why he seemed depressed.

"Millions of men are dying who could be saved if we had a better method of treatment," stated Carrel flatly.

"What do you need to find such a method?"

"I need to be free from this routine, to gather about me some choice men, especially a qualified chemist, and I need to have a laboratory. This laboratory would need to be near the front lines in order to begin the treatment at the first stages of infection."

"And if you had all that, do you think you could solve the problem?"

"I think I could."

That was enough for James Hyde. Without hesitating he interrupted his trip and went to see General Meunier, the military Governor of Lyon, who granted Major Alexis Carrel a leave. Hyde and Carrel drove across France to Bordeaux, the temporary location of the French Government due to the advance of the Germans. Hyde knew Millerand, president of the Council and foreign minister, and in one day Carrel was granted an interview with him and with the Inspector General of the Health Services. Both listened with interest to Carrel's proposals, and Millerand responded with enthusiasm: "You are probably on the right track, but I fear I won't be able to meet all your needs—for a hospital, yes, but for a laboratory, no. Let me know as soon as possible the size of the hospital and the staff you need and I will try to arrange it. Perhaps you can obtain the necessary research funds from your American Institute. While you are waiting, I think it would be good for you to visit the front to see first hand the conditions under which the men are wounded and treated."

With this encouragement and support Carrel immediately left on a tour of the front. He was given a car with chauffeur, and the yellow travel card which permitted passage throughout France without interruption. He visited French and Belgian hospitals and British installations and found great variation in quality of care and of organization. He met for the first time the respected Belgian surgeon Depage who was in the process of organizing a traveling hospital on the seacoast near Furnes, precisely 12 kilometers from the line of fire. Just before Christmas he returned to Paris for a few days, then made a second tour of the front in the eastern sector. He had breakfast at Chalons-sur-Marne, and a few kilometers further witnessed near Sainte-Menchould, for the first time, the straw huts made by soldiers. As he was driven through the village, a distant cannon roared; a shell fell nearby, killing a woman and wounding several other people. On December 26th he met Bunau-Varilla, ordinance officer of the Army of Gerand, who was en route for the trenches. The Garibaldians had been fighting since early morning. Carrel arrived in the middle of the Argonne forest where the general of the division had set up his command post. French and German shells whined as they crossed each other overhead. Carrel watched the battle from beneath the trees. Returning, he helped two Garibaldians who were going to the command post for help. He bandaged their wounds and examined the recent wounds of several injured soldiers being carried away on stretchers. In the afternoon he visited the hospital of Dr. Robert Proust which consisted of 100 beds in a small castle, and which he found well-organized. He returned by Clermont-en-Argonne where he saw a hospital in a former old peoples' home with no apparatus for sterilization.

On December 27 he visited another hospital at Islettes which was even worse. The rooms were dirty, there were no operating rooms, and no buckets. Bandages that were removed from dirty wounds were simply thrown on the floor.

Carrel returned to Paris and wrote a blistering report to the Ministry of Health. He was critical of the lack of directives, each surgeon treating wounds in his own way. One surgeon irrigated wounds with a solution of table salt, another used alcohol, one ether, another iodine. One surgical team plunged a red hot iron into the depths of the wound. All was confusion and lack of organization.

At about this time Carrel wrote a friend, "The former valor and fortitude of the French has suddenly reappeared. I hope that the young generation comes out of this war revitalized. That which I told you about French medicine these last years is unfortunately verified. They didn't predict any of this. They are ignorant of everything. Men are dying everywhere of typhoid fever and tetanus because they weren't vaccinated and we don't possess the anti-tetanus serum." Later to another friend he wrote, "It is necessary that the neutrals know what sort of civilization Germany proposes for the world. If they could really know the way in which the Germans are fighting and committing unpardonable crimes. I'm completely stupified by seeing that this country of scholars, for whom I have the most profound admiration, can reconcile this enormous intellectual development with a morality worthy of the most ignorant barbarians. A race which produced men such as Emile Fisher and Ehrlich and so many others is now similar to the brutes of the stone age. Its civilization must be rejected as a rotten fruit. How I hope the United States will get bigger quickly in order to direct the evolution of the world toward an ideal not only intellectual and scientific but also moral."

Returning to Paris, Carrel insisted that he be allowed to establish a hospital at Compiegne, 12 or 13 kilometers from the trenches, the nearest frontal zone to Paris. Here he would have the double advantage of being able to rapidly receive the wounded but also to keep in contact with the authorities.

Carrel had been corresponding with the Rockefeller Foundation through the intermediary of its general manager, Henry James. Through the Foundation a grant was obtained to establish a laboratory. Simon Flexner, the Director of the Rockefeller Institute, found for him the ideal chemist, Henry Dakin. Dakin, a tall Englishman with a bushy moustache, had worked in the private laboratories of Christian Herter in New York and was among the most able contemporary chemists. He wanted to serve his country, but was past the maximum age permitted to be a soldier, and was on the verge of seeking a job on a farm or in a factory when the opportunity to work with Carrel presented itself. He left for France at once.

Near Compiegne, on the edge of the forest, the luxury hotel Rond-Royal which had belonged to Louis-Philippe and Napoleon III was requisitioned. It was very satisfactory. There were immense rooms, a long hall and a dining room on the first floor, with painted ceilings, carpeted floors, and beautiful curtains. The bedrooms on the second floor, still containing the original furniture, served the wounded officers, and the most seriously injured of all ranks. Rows of iron cots were placed in the large first floor rooms. The medical staff resided on the second floor, while the nurses were housed in a nearby villa which also served as the kitchen. This became temporary hospital number 21, which contained the very important chemical and bacteriological laboratories, an animal and a radiological laboratory. The laboratories were subsidized by the Rockefeller Foundation which controlled their scientific activities. The rest of the hospital was under the jurisdiction of the French Military Health Service. Several competent surgeons were assigned to the hospital, Dr. Bernoud, an army Captain was assigned the administrative details, Dr. G. Dehelly from Le Havre who had visited Carrel in New York, and several others from time to time. In the radiology laboratory Dr. Joubert de Beaujeu was in charge. The bacteriology division was directed by Prof. A. Vincent from the Colonial troops, while biologist Lecomte du Nouy, a student of Louis de Broglie, carried on the animal experimental work aided by Miss A. Hartman and Miss Lilly from the Rockefeller Institute. Madame Carrel and Mademoiselle Weilman directed a group of 15 or 16 nurses; some were American and Canadian, but the majority were from Lausanne, Switzerland. All were very conscientious and efficient. An American Catholic woman who had lost her son visited with the wounded soldiers, brought them gifts from Americans and performed functions that would now be called social services.

During the first six or eight months after the establishment of the laboratory at Compiegne, Dakin tested over two hundred antiseptic solutions, trying to find the one that would destroy bacteria and dissolve dead tissue and pus without causing irritation or destruction to normal tissue or skin. He finally settled on hypocholorite of soda, an old germicidal agent which he so modified that it lost most of its irritating tendency and yet retained its germicidal quality.

During this time Carrel was working out the best method of applying this antiseptic agent to the most serious deeply lacerated wounds. He finally became satisfied that the ideal technique was one that allowed intermittent irrigation of the depths of the wound with carefully placed rubber tubes. Dakin's solution, as it came to be called, was suspended over the wounded soldier in a bottle and allowed to flow out through glass distributing tubes with many branches, each leading to a separate zone of the wound. The skin around the wound was protected by compresses of vaseline gauze. A pinchcock on the distributing tube allowed drop by drop adjustment of the speed of irrigation. The care required in the careful fixing of the tubes demanded much time and qualified personnel. The major disadvantage of the method was the fact that it demanded more care, precision, and personnel and equipment than were usually available under wartime conditions. In addition Carrel stipulated that a bacteriological smear be taken daily from every wound and that surgical closure of the wound not be carried out until the smears taken from the wound showed almost complete absence of bacteria.

A former nurse later recounted that "Dr. Carrel would come in the afternoon into the ward to examine a particularly bad wound to see if the drains were well disposed. He was very meticulous and rarely satisfied. He would enter briskly by the garden door and would go immediately to the bed which interested him. Very rarely, he assisted with dressings which were always done by surgeons. One time a wounded soldier mistook him for a priest because he always dressed in a black blouse and wore a little white cap."

One of the doctors wrote of Carrel: "His face was round, full shaven which made one of our frequent visitors on seeing him for the first time ask 'Is that your priest?' His attitude and his simple gestures were very sober, his voice was soft and contained. Behind his glasses he had two brilliant eyes. When people would question him, sometimes with naive questions, his face would light up, as he spoke with confidence of his belief in the new technique. He has a very creative mind with the ability of seeing everything from a new angle. He has a certain timidity about him, yet he can get irritated very suddenly. He has real emotions toward the suffering and cannot relax until the suffering is appeased. He doesn't have much taste for joking but he is capable of bursting out laughing at something funny. Every morning there is a long and detailed visit by the service surgeon. He examines each wound very closely, carefully distributes the irrigation tubes and proceeds to take bacteriological samples. Dr. Carrel is usually in the back of the always numerous visitors in a long black shirt and a white cap, chatting with one or the other and getting nearer to look at a wound that interests him particularly. He will take out his eyeglasses and lean over, his nose nearly on the wound."

During the first few months after establishment of Temporary Hospital number 21, Carrel was euphoric. He wrote: "The situation is favorable; my collaborators are very competent, they administer the hospital admirably, the ambulances are excellent. We have excellent nurses and my wife has organized them like an American hospital."

When otherwise unoccupied, Carrel often went to the front lines to help collect the wounded. He wrote many impressions in his notebooks such as "War is something much more frightening and absurd than I had thought. Men die with unequal courage. Women and mothers don't complain. The spectacle that our hospital represents these days is at the same time deplorable and heroic. For a long time I hated to believe the atrocities committed by the Germans in Belgium. Today I am sure that they were committed in a fashion even more barbarous than the wild tribes in Central Africa."

Gradually the method of Carrel and the solutions of Dakin improved. On May 1, 1915, he wrote in his notebook, "We are going to, perhaps, be able to disinfect the wounds." Another note dated June 6, 1915 reads: "We have obtained admirable results. If Mr. Rockefeller could see the wounded in our hospital, he would certainly experience much pleasure in contemplating that which only a small amount of his money has produced. Dakin works superbly. I am very grateful to Dr. Flexner for having sent him to me."

All through June the method continued to work wonderfully —this method would become known as the Carrel-Dakin technique. Their reputation extended further and further; they became the subject of discussion in the ambulances at the front, in the hospitals of the interior and even in foreign hospitals. They were visited in April by Harvey Cushing, the famous American surgeon and in June by Almoth Wright the biologist, now in the uniform of an English colonel. In August they received a visit from Dr. William Walsh, the eminent bacteriologist, and one of the founders of the Rockefeller Institute. Many studies were carried out along with the treatment of the wounded. The biologist Lecomte du Nouy became interested in the mathematical study of the speed of healing under various conditions. He developed a technique of making daily prints on transparent cellophane sheets of the exact area of the wound which he could measure with a planimeter and calculate accurately the curve of healing. Carrel occupied himself with other problems of the wounded such as the treatment of shock, the replacement of blood by transfusion. Since blood banks and blood preservation had not yet been developed, transfusions could only be given directly from donor to recipient. This was done occasionally from artery to vein with the Ellsberg nozzle or Tichier tubes, later with paraffin syringes.

As the fame of the hospital grew, so did resentment and opposition. In England, Almoth Wright wrote on April 24, 1915, without examining the facts, "If an efficient antiseptic for serious wounds were ever found, it would be announced in all the evening and morning papers." Other noted surgeons such as Burghard, Leishman, Sir B. Moynihan, were also skeptical. But it was at the French Academy of Medicine and the Society of Surgery in Paris that the bitterest criticisms arose. One group of surgeons claimed not only that hypoclorite did not kill bacteria, but actually provided them a convenient culture medium. The bitterest comment of all came from Professor Broca who asked, "Why all this amazement about Mr. Carrel who is only a physiologist and not a surgeon? He does not deserve such publicity as the recent newspaper article entitled, 'The American Vasco de Gama debarking on an unknown land.' No one needs to be a member of an Institute, even the Rockefeller, to do what he had done."

Carrel assuredly had a gift for angering his colleagues. He provided a perfect target. The French Surgeons became even more aroused when they received a circular, edited by Tuffier, consultant surgeon to the Army, and signed by General Chavasse which recommended to the military surgeons the principles of treatment of Carrel. As a result, Tuffier and Pozzi, who believed in the Carrel-Dakin method, were treated inhospitably when they toured the hospitals near the front lines. Carrel himself experienced this extreme bitterness. He was deeply disturbed, not so much by the criticism as by the bitterness it revealed. He made no public reply other than in the preface to a book that he and Dakin were writing at this time. Drily he asserted: "The theories and experiments published these last few months at the Academy of Medicine and the Society of Surgery have taught us that antiseptics cannot sterilize wounds. A Professor at the University of Paris has even demonstrated to the members of the

Figure 10. A Nurse using a pinch-cock to control the rate of flow of Dakin's antiseptic solution into an infected wound.

scholarly societies that, not only do the antiseptics not kill the microbes, but favor their development. However, these wounds, instead of following this doctrine have continued to be sterilized under the influence of the substances. This is not the first time in the history of medicine that the facts have defied the theories upon which they are based. It is therefore necessary to throw out the theory and to look beyond at what actually occurs."

In his private letters, he expressed himself more vehemently. "The Institute and the Academy felt insulted because we have done what they should have done. They are nearly all against me. I am proud of it. Unfortunately, many will lose their limbs and their life because of the vanity and incompetence of these French surgeons." Two months later he wrote, "Most of the French surgeons don't even want to look at what we are doing. They would prefer that the wounded suffer, die, or become disabled rather than admit that someone besides themselves has found something useful. This demonstrates that science should never be officialized in the form of an Academy. When men of Science adopt the habits of men of Religion, they immobilize science in rigid rules and progress stops."

All was not bad however; there were compensations. On the fifth of August 1915 he received the Legion of Honor from the French Army. In 1916 in the course of a visit to the Belgian hospital of his friend Depage at La Panne, he received from King Albert the Medal of Officer of the Order of Leopold.

Finally the tide of opinion among the French profession began to turn in his favor. It began with Professor E. Quenu, a deeply honest man, who decided to make a personal visit and inspection at a center where the Carrel-Dakin method was being used. He returned convinced in its favor and dared to make known his opinion. Others soon joined him.

At the end of 1916 inter-allied surgical conferences were held at which the Carrel-Dakin method was adopted as the approved treatment of infected wounds. It was there that Sir Almoth Wright had the generosity to renounce his earlier affirmation in declaring that the most important contribution to surgical technology since the beginning of the war had been the method of Carrel. Sir Anthony Bowlby, an English Army surgeon, ex-

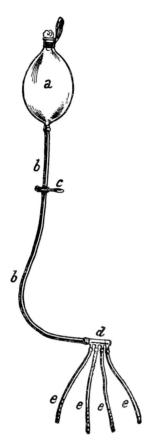

Figure 11. *Carrel's Irrigation Apparatus.* The reservoir (a) for Dakin's Solution held one liter which was delivered through the main distributing tube (b) controlling the rate of delivery by a metal pinchcock. A glass tube with multiple openings then led the fluid to the final distributing tubes which were closed at the distal end but perforated with small openings along the sides.

pressed the opinion that everywhere the method had been applied with precision, it had done everything the authors had predicted and had been inestimably beneficial for millions of wounded.

Even though the battle lines were fairly stable during 1915 and 1916, there were occasional episodes of excitement when the hospital at Rond-Royal seemed in danger of attack. On July 30,

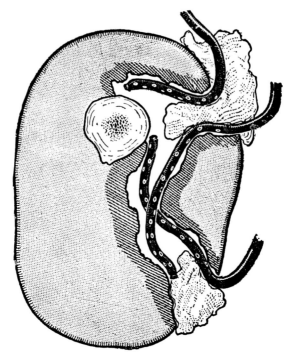

Figure 12. *Irrigation of an Irregular Wound of the Thigh.* Several irrigation tubes were placed in each wound so that Dakin's solution came in
contact with all surfaces. The wound edges were kept apart by gauze
packed loosely in the openings.

1915, the heavy bombardment of Compiegne caused a serious
alert. Carrel feared the risks run by the wounded and the personnel if they should remain. He therefore initiated preparations
for evacuation the next morning. Dr. Nimier, Director of the
Health Service, arrived with an order from General Dubois of the
6th Army not to evacuate. Carrel obeyed without comment, but
he wrote in his journal, "It is scandalous to be so daring at the
expense of the wounded." On August 27, 1915, there was another bombardment of the town. Carrel was caught in Compiegne having lunch with an English surgeon. The road was
almost impassable but he left immediately for his hospital and
found with satisfaction that everything was calm. The nurses,
accepting the danger, refused to go to the forest for shelter, but
continued their work with the wounded. On September 13, air

bombs killed 16 people and wounded 22 in the nearby village. Everything became peaceful again, but a search was ordered for another suitable place for the hospital. None was found, so they continued as before near Compiegne, even increasing the number of beds and enlarging the laboratory.

Dakin left in October 1915 for the Dardanelles to see how their prinicples of treatment were being applied in the West at the floating hospital of Charles Roux. In his absence, certain problems arose about the manufacture of the hypochlorite solution. Several months later, he returned very tired from fevers contracted during his voyage. Justifiably or not, he had come to feel that he was not receiving proper recognition for his important part in the success of this common project of treating the wounded. Once the method of production of hypochlorite solution was going well again, Dakin departed once more, returning permanently to America.

Carrel became interested in the development of a mobile hospital which would be an appendage of Rond-Royal, and which would allow him to travel with the army and be close to the sectors of battle that were most active. This would allow him an opportunity to study shock, then still a source of mystery.

At about this time he met the American architect Charles Butler, who had come to France in June 1915 to offer his services as a volunteer ambulance driver. Butler was told that there were already too many ambulance drivers, but that since he spoke French fluently and had a diploma from the Beaux Arts, he could be very helpful at the Health Bureau in Paris. It was there he and Carrel met for the first time. Carrel recognized in Butler the qualities he most respected—uprightness, unselfishness and enthusiasm. Butler had a wide experience in the construction of hospitals, and plans for the construction of a mobile hospital began immediately. They first planned to build a temporary hospital as near the front lines as possible, then to work on the idea of a truly mobile hospital. A search was begun for a suitable piece of land as near the battle lines as possible. The Duke of Uzes offered his Chateau of Lucheux, north of Doullers. General Dubail agreed, but at the end of two days' study this site was abandoned since it was divided by valleys and offered no favorable building site. Finally the mobile hospital was completed after many meetings with the Health Bureau. It consisted of a light motor surgical ambulance, with built-in autoclaves, its own power plant, a portable laboratory, and collapsible operating rooms. It was put into operation at Soissonnais in October 1917, manned by a surgeon, Dr. H. Woimant and a bacteriologist, Dr. Lechelle.

Carrel continued to be disenchanted with the caliber of French medical officers: "The medical corps is suffering from an intellectual malady which the majority of Frenchmen attain. The purely verbal education that they have received makes them take words for facts. As soon as they have spoken, they believe they have acted. They are always persuaded that what is logical is true, and that a label placed by them on something transforms that thing into whatever they desire. My compatriots, despite their intelligence, are almost unusable. Very few are capable of doing something exactly as it has been described. They experience the need to improve it. The other day I met a little doctor who sincerely believed that he knew much more chemistry than Dakin. Nevertheless, I have had great satisfaction in being able to improve the treatment of the wounded. That has made me forget a little bit the anguish of being on a drifting boat. I am very grateful to the Rockefeller Foundation for having permitted me to put in good condition a certain number of my compatriots. If the treatment had been universally applied, what economy in men and money would have been achieved. I am in France as on a desert island, heartbroken to see that my compatriots have not known how to serve themselves, or to make any progress, and that our wounded are not getting any profit from the lessons we have learned."

In the United States, meanwhile, the war was drawing ever closer. Growing tension between this country and the Central Powers reached a peak with the sinking of the "Lusitania" in May, 1915. On February 1, 1917, the Kaiser's government announced the resumption of unrestricted submarine warfare, rendering inevitable the United States' entrance into the war. Even before President Wilson's address of April 2, 1917, calling upon Congress to recognize the existence of a state of war, the

Rockefeller Institute's governing boards had begun to discuss their responsibilities in the pending crisis. One possible contribution was clear: teaching the Carrel-Dakin method to American medical officers. Flexner offered to set up a center for this purpose. Carrel was asked to return to New York on leave and the two men immediately called upon the Surgeons General of the Army and the Navy in Washington.

With a special appropriation from the Rockefeller Foundation, the Institute began a War Demonstration Hospital on June 1, 1917. Planned to imitate conditions near the front, the project also offered a good opportunity to experiment with designs for temporary hospitals based on European experience rather than on installations that had heretofore served the Army's needs. Carrel's architect friend Charles Butler, who had studied British and French military hospitals as well as planning Carrel's mobile hospital, was called back to New York to design the War Demonstration Hospital. The sixteen portable wooden buildings, occupying the whole southwest corner of the Rockefeller Institute's grounds, were completed in six weeks—a remarkable feat, testifying to skillful planning and enthusiastic cooperation between architect, builders and the building manager of the Institute. The hospital consisted of two wards of twenty-five beds each and an operating pavilion with all the necessary facilities and dormitories for the entire personnel.

The War Demonstration Hospital was staffed by both French and American military surgeons. The former, four in all, headed by Carrel, were detached by the French Army from the group he had trained at Compiegne; the latter, together with a number of bacteriologists and chemists, were assigned by the Surgeon General of the U.S. Army. The first patients were civilians suffering from a variety of infected wounds; these were replaced, after American forces entered combat, by soldier patients sent home from France. Twice monthly from August 2, 1917 to March 29, 1919 a new class of medical officers came for two weeks' instruction in the Carrel-Dakin method. In addition, specialists were given short courses in the chemical preparation of Dakin's solution and in the bacteriological testing and control of the surgical treatment.

Figure 13. *The War Demonstration Hospital.* The sixteen portable wooden buildings occupied the southwest corner of the Rockefeller Institute's grounds. Here between 1917 and 1919 American Army surgeons were trained in the Carrel-Dakin technique of management of war wounds.

Carrel returned to France in the spring of 1918. The hospital at Compiegne continued to operate calmly and methodically. The uninterrupted pilgrimage of great names in French and allied surgery testified to its success. Carrel busied himself experimenting with new modes of treatment conceived and studied in New York. He frequently went to the front to study extreme emergencies, and to observe the functioning of his motor hospital. He was at the front when a catastrophe occurred at Rond-Royal. In the early winter of 1918 the Russian debacle had liberated many German divisions. On March 21 the German offensive of Ludendorff had begun. Six thousand cannons were fired unceasingly upon the English Army, and through a fog the assault began. At Rond-Royal the balconies of the hospital trembled with the continuous thundering of the guns in the distance. Madame Carrel met anxiously with the chiefs of the Services to decide what measures should be taken. Evacuation was discussed, but there were so many seriously wounded that this was deemed impossible. Besides, there had been no evacuation order. The night of March 23 was clear and a full moon illuminated the surrounding woods. It was 4:30 in the morning, and only the night nurses were awake. On the top floor a night nurse had just cared for a very seriously injured soldier with a wound of the thigh. Crossing in front of the window she glanced toward the sky and noticed a great black body crossing in front of the moon. It was, without doubt, a plane returning from battle. She noticed it approaching the hospital, then to her horror she realized it was a German bomber. At that moment the alarm sounded; everyone was asked to go to the first floor. Dr. Daufresne ran to the third floor and called the missing nurse. There was an explosion which shook all the furniture and cut off his words. A bomb had detonated in the courtyard, breaking down all the doors and raising a cloud of dust and fire. The nurse cried "But we can't move this man, I'm going to stay with him." She piled mattresses around the cot of the unfortunate and immobilized soldier. There was another frightening explosion which seemed very near, followed immediately by a wall falling through and the front of the building collapsing. The nurse thought the end had come and tightly closed her eyes. Two more explosions occurred one after the other, and another piece of wall fell. The third floor tilted at a dangerous angle; dust and smoke made breathing difficult. A few seconds later, the last two bombs detonated harmlessly in the nearby woods. The plane, having discharged its cargo, flew back towards the German lines.

The wounded and personnel, miraculously, were uninjured, unharmed, but around them lay destruction and ruin. Only the skeleton of the hospital remained. Later that day evacuation began by train and by ambulance. In the absence of Carrel, Daufresne was the last to leave the building. He stooped to pick up a bottle in the debris, "the first sample of Dakin's solution."

At first the refugees were installed in a chateau at Lagny-sur-Marne. Everything had to be put together again and reorganized, but the rapidly progressing offensive blocked any such possibilities. There was no question of comfort, so they organized themselves as well as they could. Wounded abounded and there was much work to do. Carrel rejoined his hospital group and worked with them until the situation quieted a little. The following months were extremely active as the battle increased in furor. Finally with the full force of the American counterattack, the Germans began to retreat. Peace arrived November 11, 1918.

In the last year of the war, transport of the wounded improved, so that they reached hospitals more quickly. Thus there were fewer massive infections, and wounds could be closed immediately after debridement. In time of peace, there were still fewer occasions for combating deep purulent infections. Civilian surgeons did not feel it necessary to maintain the special apparatus, the chemical and bacterial control, the supply of precisely buffered Dakins solution, and the constant attention that went into successful operation of the Carrel-Dakin method at Compiegne and later in New York. The method therefore did not take hold in civilian major surgery, though Dakin's solution was long used as a disinfectant for trivial wounds. More than twenty years were to elapse before the problem of wound infection was revolutionized by the discovery of penicillin and other antibiotics.

After the armistice Carrel and Lecomte du Nouy set up a small laboratory in a wooden barrack near Saint-Cloud where they completed experiments begun the previous year and which thirty years later were considered remarkable in their foresight. They investigated the importance of blood volume in shock, the physical and chemical properties of resuscitating fluids (such as the major role of protein molecules), the balance of acid and base ions, and the metabolism of carbohydrates. Then Carrel closed his notebook, his warbook, covered with hurried lines, erasures, sketches, chemical formulas, figures and notes. On December 15, 1918 he wrote, "I have finished my experiments at Saint Cloud. My next return to New York will be toward the 15th of January. I have succeeded in finding the greatest part of that which I wanted. It is too bad that it is six months too late." He also commented in another letter, "In France there is beginning again as before the same method, the same spirit of narrowness and conservatism and injustice."

One of his contemporaries, Professor J. Lepine, stated, "After the war Carrel wasn't French anymore, as he had never really been but he was even less exclusively a scholar. The horror of the disaster that humanity underwent during the war was a perpetual torment to him. Many times during the weeks following the armistice he considered remaining in France to dedicate his energy and experience to the service of his country, but he recognized very quickly that it wasn't time yet for political philosophers."

# CHAPTER VII

 POST WAR YEARS

At the Rockefeller Institute a glorious welcome awaited the return of the "Frenchman." The services rendered by Major Carrel to the Allied Armies were greatly appreciated. The U.S. Army recognized him with a Distinguished Service Certificate; John D. Rockefeller recommended to the Board of the Rockefeller Institute that Carrel's Department of Experimental Surgery be given additional space and equipment.

Alexis and Anne Carrel resumed the rhythm of the life they had lived before the War. They resided at the Blackstone Hotel for several years, then moved to the Garden City Hotel. Madame Carrel often accompanied her husband on his medical trips and to scientific meetings. After 1926, however, she began to spend more and more time in France. It is not clear exactly why she did so except that she felt the climate, the crowds and the heat of New York to be interfering with her health. In spite of their physical separation, Carrel rendered her all the respect and tenderness that had been without object since the death of his mother. Nevertheless their matrimonial life was subordinate to his vocation and career.

Carrel continued his custom of spending three months each summer in France. He returned faithfully to Lyon for a few weeks. Since the War his name had become a source of pride to all the people of the city. Part of each summer was spent at La Batie with the memories of his youth, and the remainder at Madame Carrel's family home in Anjou at the Chateau du Molines.

More and more the Carrels felt the need for a retreat of their own, away from crowded sidewalks, automobile traffic and urban noise. They decided to seek solitude in a relatively secluded corner of France. The regions of la Creuse and Beaujolais were thoroughly explored. Carrel then met Anatole Le Braz, who was lecturing in New York. Le Braz knew and loved the province of Bretagne along the Atlantic coast of France, and he described its charm, its beautiful scenery and its isolated and sparsely populated area. Dr. Eberling, Carrel's young associate at the Institute told him about an island along the northern coast. Decidedly, it was there that the Carrels should look for their retreat. Madame Carrel went to Bretagne, received more information from Le Braz, and explored the Island of Saint Gildas. An offer was made its owner, but the island was not for sale. Negotiations continued for two years. Finally in 1922, the Carrels acquired the property, paying for it largely with the money which remained from the Nobel Prize. The island was named for the saint who had evangelized Bretagne; it had a balmy climate, much more temperate than the area surrounding it. Vegetation was sparse on this isolated spot, which proved a wonderful location for the solitude they sought. The island could only be reached by small boat from the mainland; except at low tide when one could walk from the mainland and between islands. In the center of the island stood a very old but sturdy house of masonry, with a disjointed flagstone floor. It was the ideal place to find calm and solitude, a perfect hermitage. It was here that the Carrels spent much of their summers for the next twenty years, and where Carrel stated that he wished to be buried. Very few people visited the island. Carrel loved to walk out and sit on the high rocks and dream for hours as he gazed out upon the horizon.

Each September Carrel returned by boat to New York. His architect friend, Charles Butler, who crossed the Atlantic with him several times, described how Alexis would sometimes go to the bar in the evening to watch the passengers drink their whisky and cocktails. He would sit wrinkling his eyes and observing in silence the progressive effect of the beverages on the physical aspects and behavior of people. He was from his youth distressed by the destruction of lives by alcoholism, which he noticed in both France and America. In his articles and lectures he deplored the evils of alcohol and its debilitating consequences on both the individual moral fiber and on the human race.

As Madame Carrel left France less and less over the years, her husband rented a small penthouse on the tenth floor at 56

East 86th street in New York. It was a very modest apartment, almost monastic, whose only luxury was a circular terrace which overlooked Central Park. He had no works of art on the walls, kept no radio, and asked very few if any of his friends to visit him there. His long nights alone he spent reading, studying, writing or reflecting. He usually went to bed about one o'clock and seldom slept more than five hours. He would then arise at six o'clock and walk for several miles around the reservoir in Central Park. His social life consisted of occasional dinners with friends at the Century Club on Fifth Avenue or on weekends at the Piping Rock Club on Long Island. His friends included Frederick Coudert, Forrest Buckmitest, Cornelius Clifford, a Communist Priest who had been banished from the Jesuit Order, but who still had a small parish in New Jersey, and Boris Bakmetiff, a former professor of fluid mechanics in Moscow, who had been the last ambassador of the Czar to the United States before the Russian Revolution. Also among his close acquaintances were Professors Samuel Butler and Woolridge of Columbia University, the ex-French minister P. Reynaud, J. Maritain the German philosopher, and Albert Einstein, as well as Justice Cardoza of the United States Supreme Court. This group came to be called "the Philosophers." What wide ranging discussions they had, what a sounding board against which to test new ideas and theories!

In spite of these highly valued friendships, Carrel remained basically a monastic, a loner. He frequently felt the need to escape from New York for a few days or a week to a deserted out-of-season hotel. In 1924 he visited Southern Pines, North Carolina, in 1932 Woodstock, Vermont, and in the fall of 1937 and 1938 with Madame Carrel he traveled to Florida. He wrote, "Periods of solitude and of silence are indispensible. Each one of us must submit ourselves to such periods from time to time. We can say that one can recharge himself with energy, especially when he adds moderate exercise and a little bit of sunshine. The Americans have chosen the opposite route, life always in a group, with complete rejection of meditation and inner discipline."

Again he wrote, "I am in the woods of North Carolina where there are trees, flowers, and the air is not saturated with the vapors of gasoline. In New York the life of humans is becoming pitiful. We find ourselves in the same situation as the microbes, locked up in a certain culture poisoned by the products of our activity."

Alexis Carrel's most elaborate venture into the field of cancer research was known to few even within the Rockefeller Institute. Carrel had long been fascinated by the problem of malignancy— his doctoral thesis in Lyon concerned thyroid cancer. The tissue culture methods developed in his laboratory enabled him and his associates to carry out or cooperate in many experiments into the behavior of cancer cells in the test tube and of nutritional and environmental factors which affect their multiplication and growth. Eventually, he conceived ideas of his own as to the cause of cancer and was given sufficient financial support by Flexner to develop these ideas. There is very little in the records of the Rockefeller Institute to document these efforts. Flexner only made vague mention in his 1930 account of the Rockefeller Institute of Carrel's view that heredity and environmental factors played a part in the susceptibility to cancer. Carrel had observed certain villages of French peasants and fishermen in which the annual death rate from cancer was 4 to 5 per thousand and others where it was as low as 0.5 per thousand. He believed the great difference between the cancer incidence in people of identical heritage and way of life was due to a difference in their diet. There was a higher cancer rate in those villages which had modernized their diet—which now consisted of white bread; margarine and canned foods—believed to contain possibly harmful substances with less fresh vegetables, butter, milk and eggs than the usual diet of French villages. Carrel believed that this modernized diet made the tissues of the individuals more susceptible to cancer.

To test this theory a huge "mousery" was built far from public view on an upper floor of the powerhouse. Four pure-bred strains of mice were maintained in this air conditioned, glass roofed structure. In part of the area there were four large deep bins containing soil in which the mice ran wild in burrows under relatively natural conditions. Some mice were fed on canned food and purchased grains while others were fed fresh untreated foods. Carrel even tried to grow various grains in the bins to provide fresh food, but these efforts failed. At its peak the mouse population reached 55,000. It was quite an expensive venture, costing $70,000 in 1928 to construct the mousery and $20,000 for each of the next five years to operate. The project was not funded after 1933 for reasons that are not clear. One opinion of the cause of failure of this experiment was the fact that the mice in the big bins defeated the researchers by dying in their burrows where they could not be examined after death. Others believe that failure was due to the records that were too voluminous for analysis. Flexner, who was usually very enthusiastic about Carrel's projects, never made a formal report to the Institute Board on the scientific achievements of this project. He commented later that he had authorized the experiment because he felt that when one of the Institute's most productive investigators wanted to test one of his ideas, it was important that the Director support him and not discourage him by prejudging his hypothesis.

Carrel's earlier success with organ transplantation had been frustrated by the failure caused by rejection. In spite of his ingenious surgical methods of suturing vessels which allowed an organ from one animal to be transplanted to another, this resulted in only short survival of the organ. Years later it was learned that rejection was due to specific antigens in animal and human blood and tissues that make the cells of one individual unacceptable in the body of another. It was already known that transfusion of blood from one individual to another might have disastrous results, unless the patients were carefully matched within the four major blood groups recently discovered by Landsteiner, Carrel's colleague at the Rockefeller Institute. Landsteiner also demonstrated that the incompatibility of organs is far more specific than that between blood groups. Very minute differences, still incompletely defined, in the protein matrix of all human cells distinguish each individual from all other individuals, even his parents and siblings, except identical twins.

Hoping that it would be possible to cultivate transplantable organs without a donor's incompatible antigens, Carrel tried to extend the culture of cells to that of whole organs. As years went by he became less interested in the surgical implications of tissue and organ culture and more interested in the physiological possibilities provided by these techniques. Biological problems came more and more to dominate his thinking, while those of a surgical technician receded. By the time he was ready to attempt the cultivation of whole organs, he was convinced that the physiological study of nutrition, respiration, secretion and regulation of function would be more important results of this new method than would be the improvement in the possibilities of surgical organ transplantation. He felt that science might learn "how the organs develop from the organism and how the organism grows, ages, heals its wounds, resists disease and adapts itself to changing environment." "The ultimate goal of the culture of organs is to obtain this new knowledge and to pursue it through the complexity of its unpredictable consequences." Carrel, in his fifties, was venturing like an enthusiastic young researcher into one of the most difficult fields of all science and he hoped to get answers to age-old questions with this new method. Physiologists had worked for a century on methods for keeping fragments of animal tissues and isolated organs alive and functioning outside the animals body so they could be studied. Langandorf had shown that a frog heart will beat for hours in an oxygenated solution of salts in the proper proportions, with a chemical buffer to keep the solution from becoming too acid and a little sugar added to supply energy. The heart finally stops beating either because of lack of adequate nourishment or because of contaminating infection.

This physiological bath can supply temporary nutrition to the cells of the frog heart because the heart walls are so thin they can be permeated directly by the fluids. Organs that are thicker must have their cells supplied by pumping fluids directly into the primary artery of the organ. This technique, labeled organ perfusion, was first used in Leipzig in about 1860 in the laboratory of the physiologist Carl Ludwig. One of his pupils kept a liver alive by perfusing it outside the body long enough to demonstrate that the liver could still produce urea which appeared in the perfusion fluid. It was found by early workers in the field of perfusion that organs functioned better if the fluid was pumped through the vessels in pulses similar to the heart beat. With pulsatile pumps, isolated organs were kept alive and functioning for several hours and much was learned about gland secretions, nutritive requirements and waste disposal by these brief experiments, before the organs deteriorated. Before long-term survival could be achieved, many more factors would have to be controlled. The fluid for artificial perfusion must be carefully filtered free of floating particles such as clumps of blood cells which might plug capillary vessels as small as $\frac{1}{4000}$ inch in diameter. Temperature and the balance of acidity vs. alkalinity (pH) must be carefully adjusted as must the osmotic pressure and oxygen content of the fluid. Even the pulse rate and range of pressure pulse must be regulated, but most important of all, the perfused organ must be carefully protected from infection by bacteria.

Realizing the importance of aseptic technique, Carrel, with one of his technicians, Heinz Rosenberger, in 1929 began to develop and construct a sterilizable glass perfusion pump which operated by a magnet outside the glass chamber. He added Dakin's solution to the perfusion fluid; still his efforts met with failure due to infection.

Fate intervened in Carrel's behalf at this unfortunate stage in the form of Charles A. Lindbergh, who volunteered his assistance. A relative of Lindbergh's, following a bout with pneumonia, developed "lesions of the heart." Lindbergh asked physician friends if such lesions could be removed surgically and was informed that an operation on the heart was impossible. He knew little about the biological aspects of such problems, but being keenly interested in mechanical developments, he considered whether it would be possible to construct an artificial heart which could maintain circulation so that surgeons could stop the heart while operating upon it. One physician friend with whom he discussed this possibility introduced him to Carrel. Upon learning of the difficulties Carrel was having with his perfusion pump, Lindbergh agreed to try to design an improved pump and became a volunteer assistant in Carrel's laboratory.

Lindbergh had made his pioneering trans-Atlantic flight from New York to Paris only three years before and was still a public figure who excited intense public interest. He tried to slip into

Carrel's laboratory by a side door for his first visit, but the news slipped out and the windows along his path were filled with curious and admiring technicians and secretaries. There was at first some resentment on the part of senior scientists that Carrel would allow an amateur to work with him among the select ranks of scientific researchers. There was also some fear of sensational publicity. As Lindbergh's presence became familiar around the Institute, and as the scientists came to appreciate his modesty and discretion, all objections disappeared and he was held in quiet respect by the professional investigators. He was treated by the administration of the Institute as Carrel's guest and received no pay or official recognition. No one at the Institute would discuss his presence with the press.

Lindbergh's first pump was a spiral glass tube mounted upright on a motor-driven base. As the coiled tube was swung in a circle on its fixed base (like a man waving a flag with his upraised arms) fluid was made to flow upward along the spiral to a reservoir, and then down through a vertical tube and a cannula inserted into the main artery of the organ to be perfused. This pump did not pulsate and did not develop enough pressure, and insertion of the organ into the chamber was difficult without also introducing infection. In spite of this, Carrel and Lindbergh were able to perfuse with serum a segment of animal carotid artery for one month without infection. After four years of work, in 1934, Lindbergh conceived an improved method of transmitting power into a sterile system. He found that large volumes of air could be forced through sterile non-absorbent cotton balls loosely packed in a glass bulb. The cotton removed all bacteria from the incoming air. He proved that cotton could sterilize flowing air by forcing air from the piped laboratory supply through such a bulb and into a sterile broth culture medium, in which no bacteria grew after a month on continuous flow. When gas was used to exert pulsating pressures, the resulting flow of perfusing medium was much more like the natural flow of blood through a body than a mechanically-activated (i.e. piston acting within the medium) flow would have been.

Finally in the spring of 1935, a satisfactory model was successfully used. A rotating valve produced a pulse in the compressed air used to drive the pump. Pulsating pressure was transmitted indirectly to the "control gas" which was a mixture of oxygen, nitrogen and carbon dioxide. This gas performed two functions—to circulate and to oxygenate the perfusion fluid and was essentially the first pump-oxygenator. The isolated organ came in contact only with glass and the perfusion fluid. Temperature and pressure (flow was regulated by pressure) could be controlled from outside. The perfusing fluid was automatically filtered with each passage and could be renewed without bacterial contamination. It required only twenty minutes for Carrel to excise and insert an animal organ such as a kidney, heart or spleen. The pump was made in one piece of autoclavable Pyrex glass by the Rockefeller Institute's ingenious glass blower, Otto Hopf. Another Institute staff worker, Lillian E. Baker, made a careful study of the composition of perfusion fluids to develop the most nutritious one possible.

The thyroid gland of a cat was successfully perfused for eighteen days beginning on April 5, 1935. At the end of that time much of its tissue appeared partially preserved and pieces of it, when transferred to tissue culture, grew epithelial cells proving it was still alive.

Many other organs were "cultured" over the next few years. Hearts were kept beating for several days, Fallopian tubes continued to show peristaltic movement, ovaries increased in size. Kidneys proved to be more delicate, surviving only one day of perfusion, but producing urine copiously for a few hours before degeneration started. There was some fragmentary evidence of even more specialized physiological activity persisting in isolated perfused organs such as production of insulin by the pancreas and antibodies by the spleen. The average duration of organ perfusion was about one week but a thyroid gland was perfused for thirty days with survival of some of its cells. Over one thousand experiments were conducted with the Lindbergh pump and much was learned about the physiological requirements of isolated organs. Red blood cells were added to the perfusing fluid in some experiments to increase the oxygen carrying capacity of the fluid but this failed because the red cells fragmented (hemolysed) from the mechanical trauma they received.

Several laboratories in Europe and America experimented with organ culture, but it was never widely used. Research in biology was moving away from the study of whole organs and more toward the study of individual cells. Researchers interested in the investigation of cell function and structure found that an organ could be studied no better when isolated than in the living animal. Although perfused organs survived surprisingly well, all began to show progressive degenerative changes in a few days, edema fluid filled tissue spaces, arteries became calcified, connective tissue cells outgrew the more specialized cells.

Several dozen Lindbergh pumps had been built between 1935 and 1938. These were gradually abandoned for the reasons stated above, but also because Carrel retired in 1939 and World War II directed scientific work in other directions. Twenty years later, in the mid-1950's, the same principles were to be used for total body perfusion in the development of pump oxygenators for open heart surgery, Lindbergh's original concept that stimulated his interest. In the 1960's, organ perfusion began to be used again to preserve donor organs, such as the kidney and liver, removed immediately after death and maintained for a few hours in good condition until a patient who badly needed such a transplant could be put to sleep and prepared for implantation of the organ.

Organ perfusion failed to be useful in the area of physiology for which it was intended, but years later proved valuable in surgical fields and for purposes deemed incidental at the time it was introduced. Tissue culture, Carrel's earlier contribution, suffered the same fate; a technique devised to study limited and specialized biological problems is now essential to the cultivation of cell dependent viruses, for instance, polio, and to prepare vaccines against them.

The public press eventually realized the drama of the young aviator working with the distinguished scientist to develop an artificial heart pump. Journalists obtained an accurate description of his early pump in *Science* in 1931 and his final version in the *Journal of Experimental Medicine* in 1935, and most newspaper writers wrote responsible descriptions of the work and its potentialities. Even Carrel, who stuck strictly to facts in his scientific articles, informally expressed his hopes for the future for organ

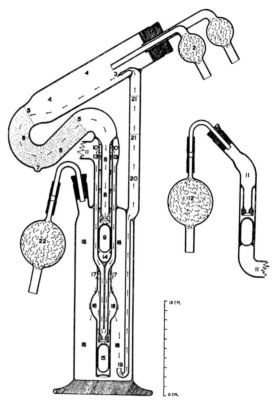

Figure 14. *The Lindbergh Apparatus for Culture of Whole Organs.* The reservoir chamber (18) was under pulsating pressure and release of the control gas passing through the cotton filter bulb. Consequently the perfusion fluid passed from the reservoir chamber (18) into the mouth of the feed tube (19) and through the feed tube (20) where it was filtered by two platinum screens (21). The fluid then passed through the cannula (3) to the organ and into the organ chamber (4). It was then pumped through a silica sand filter (6) past the upper (9) and lower (15) floating valves which prevented back flow of the fluid and then to the starting point in the reservoir chamber (18). Cotton wool in all the inlet and outlet ports (22, 12, 1, 2) kept bacteria out. The perfusion fluid was oxygenated by surface contact with the oxygen rich gas mixture used to pump the fluid around the apparatus.

perfusion and predicted storage of organs and even of temporarily removing injured organs for treatment. Sensational newspapers grossly exaggerated both Carrel's goals and accomplishments such as a description of his plans to propagate human babies in a

Figure 15. Charles Lindbergh and Alexis Carrel as they appeared on the cover of Time Magazine July 1, 1935, with their "mechanical heart."

test tube and to keep a human brain alive and thinking by perfusion.

In 1938, Lindbergh and Carrel published a book, *The Culture of Organs,* which described their work in detail. The Lindbergh pump became a popular exhibit at the New York World's Fair in 1939, where it was sponsored by a drug firm and operated by two of Carrel's former technicians. In the Fair's Hall of Medicine, perfusion of a dog's thyroid was demonstrated before large crowds.

Charles Lindbergh and his family became close personal friends of the Carrel's and in 1938 the Lindbergh family bought the island of Illiec near Saint Gildas so they could spend summer vacations together. This is a description that Lindbergh wrote of their summers together: "At the Carrel's home, one of the doors opens on a large garden surrounded by walls on three sides; the other side being open and facing the sea. Here Madame Carrel busied herself with flowers and vegetables, taking care of the fruit trees cultivated in espaliers. In his goings, in broad daylight or at twilight, one could see Carrel, his vest buttoned to his neck to protect him from the wind, walking slowly, always wearing a beret, he seemed to be freeing himself to a profound contemplation. At night at dinner time, near the chimney of the dining room made of ancient stone of Brittany, the conversation ranged from politics to ghosts. What is the best form of government of Man? The requirements and needs varied with the centuries, concluded Carrel. Was War inevitable? In Europe the situation was extremely grave. Would they be able to find again the drunken peasant who had hypnotized the dogs of St. Gildas? How explain the stories of the haunted well? Sometimes at midnight, in the light of the moon, we would walk to the well ourselves. The extraordinary surroundings of the island tended to merge the scientific with the mystical. Why require a rational explanation of all phenomena and concepts?"

CHAPTER VIII

 THE PHILOSOPHER AND MYSTIC

O VER THE YEARS, Carrel continued to meet frequently with his "philosopher" friends. These meetings were usually organized by Frederick Coudert, who admired Carrel so much that he named one of his sons Alexis Carrel Coudert. The esteem was mutual. These men felt that Carrel was an original thinker, a profound intellect with clear logic behind his opinions. In the early 1930's they began to ask that Carrel summarize his views of science and philosophy in a book. They assured him that the popular interest in this subject, the authority of his name and his reputation would guarantee success of such a work. One of his friends wrote him in April, 1933, "The more I think about it the more I am seized with the profound conviction that a book which would summarize your thoughts and your studies is of highest importance to the world. Frankly, I do not know of anyone who could do this work besides yourself. I hope you will begin this instant; it must be done."

Under such pressure Carrel finally accepted the idea. Simon Flexner, the Director of the Rockefeller Institute, was a part of the conspiracy and provided the necessary time by ordering that Carrel's laboratory be completely painted. Carrel grumbled about not being able to pursue his experiments for a time, saying "I will not be able to do anything but return to France."

The book was written in French and took most of 1933 to complete. It was first entitled *Individual*, then *Man, the Unknown*. The English translation required almost as much care as the original work itself. The book was a tremendous publishing success, it quickly spread throughout the world and was translated into nineteen different languages and sold 900,000 copies.

The theme of the book was stated by Carrel as follows: "For the first time in the history of humanity, a crumbling civilization is capable of discerning the causes of its decay. For the first time, it has at its disposal the gigantic strength of science. Will we utilize this knowledge and this power? It is our only hope of escaping the fate common to all great civilizations of the past. Our destiny is in our hands. On the new road, we must now go forward."

*Man, the Unknown* was first of all an excellent summary in easy-to-understand language of the state of knowledge of human physiology and medicine as it existed in the mid-1930's. Carrel summarized this beautifully but stressed the vast amount of information that was still missing about man and that should be studied further. He felt that a much greater effort should be directed to the study of the mind, as well as the body, and that experimental methods must be developed to study the soul before there could be a more complete understanding of man. Only rudimentary information was available in any of these areas but he did not hesitate to express his ideas about what should be done. He expressed a strong belief in will power as a solution to character defects, yet he believed that "happiness depends on one being exactly fitted to the nature of one's work." In another passage Carrel expressed the following view about ambition: "The passion for conquest assumes diverse aspects according to individuals and circumstances. It inspires all great adventures. Such passion led Pasteur to the renovation of medicine, Mussolini to the build up of a great nation, Einstein to the creation of a universe. The same spirit drives the modern human being to robbery, murder, and to the great financial and economic enterprises characterizing our civilization. But its impulse also builds hospitals, laboratories, universities and churches. It impels men to fortune and to death, to heroism and to crime. But never to happiness."

Carrel's view on women and sex were extremely conservative even for that less liberated era. "A workman's wife can request the services of her husband every day. But the wife of an artist or of a philosopher has not the right to do so as often. It is well known that sexual excesses impede intellectual activity." Later he stated, "In reality, woman differs profoundly from man—Women should develop their aptitudes in accordance with their own nature, without trying to imitate the males. Their part in the progress of civilization is higher than that of men. They should not abandon their specific function." And again, "Women should receive a higher education, not in order to become doctors, lawyers, or professors, but to rear their offspring to be valuable human beings." Another interesting statement he made, without any supporting data was "Women who have no children are not so well balanced and become more nervous than the others."

Strong views were expressed about education: "The education dispensed by schools and universities consists chiefly in a training of the memory and of the muscles, in certain social manners, in a worship of athletics. Are such disciplines really suitable for modern men who need, above all other things, mental equilibrium, nervous stability, sound judgment, audacity, moral courage, and endurance." His comments on genius were interesting: "There is a class of men—who are indispensable to modern society. They are the men of genius. These are characterized by a monstrous growth of some of their psychological activities. A great artist, a great scientist, a great philosopher, is rarely a great man. He is generally a man of common type, with one side overdeveloped. Genius can be compared to a tumor growing upon a normal organism. These ill-balanced beings are often unhappy. But they give the entire community the benefit of their mighty impulses. Their disharmony results in the progress of civilization. Humanity has never gained anything from the efforts of the crowd. It is driven onward by the passion of a few abnormal individuals, by the flame of their intelligence, by their ideal of science, of charity, and of beauty." So it was not so much genius he advocated, as all around men. "The happiest and most useful men consist of a well-integrated whole of intellectual, moral, and organic activities. The quality of these activities, and their equilibrium, gives to such a type its superiority over the others. Their intensity determines the social level of a given individual. It makes of him a tradesman or a bank president, a little physician or a celebrated professor, a village mayor or a President."

In the realm of the mystical and spiritual, Carrel stated his strong belief in the presence of clairvoyance and mental telepathy, and his opinion that these areas should be studied much more intensively. He expressed a sincere faith in healing by prayer, and felt that the patient did not need to pray for himself or even be a believer for the faith of others to heal him. These beliefs obviously dated back to his pivotal "Voyage to Lourdes." Medical men reviewing this book were often most critical of Carrel's "gullibility" because of these statements.

Carrel was also criticized by his reviewers because of judgemental statements such as: "Why should more years be added to the life of persons who are unhappy, stupid, selfish, and useless?" And again: "The democratic principle has contributed to the collapse of civilization in opposing the development of an elite. Indeed human beings are equal. But individuals are not. The equality of their rights is an illusion. The feeble minded and the man of genius should not be equal before the law. The stupid, the unintelligent, those who are dispersed, incapable of attention, of effort, have no right to a higher education. It is absurd to give them the same electoral power as the fully developed individuals. Sexes are not equal."

His views on dealing with crime, criminals and the insane were even more shocking. "Criminality and insanity can be prevented only by a better knowledge of man; by eugenics, by changes in education and social conditions. Meanwhile, criminals have to be dealt with effectively. Perhaps prisons should be abolished. They could be replaced by smaller and less expensive institutions. The conditioning of petty criminals with the whip, or some more scientific procedure, followed by a short stay in the hospital, would probably suffice to insure order. Those who have murdered, robbed while armed with an automatic pistol or machine gun, kidnapped children, despoiled the poor of their savings, misled the public in important matters, should be humanely and economically disposed of in small euthanasic institutions supplied with proper gases. A similar treatment could be advantageously applied to the insane, guilty of criminal acts."

To his credit, Carrel felt that working men should be treated more as individuals and that dehumanizing assembly lines should be abandoned in favor of allowing factory workers to complete the production of entire articles. He made a strong plea to physicians to treat people, not diseases. "We should turn our attention toward promoting the optimum growth of the fit. By making the strong still stronger, we could effectively help the weak. For the herd always profits by the ideas and inventions of the elite."

One of Carrel's most interesting and original proposals was the creation of a scientific center for the study of man. "Such an organization would be the salvation of the white races in their staggering advance toward civilization. This thinking center would consist, as does the Supreme Court of the United States, of a few individuals; the latter being trained in the knowledge of man by many years of study. It should perpetuate itself automatically, in such a manner as to radiate ever young ideas. Democratic rulers, as well as dictators, could receive from this source of scientific truth the information that they need in order to develop a civilization really suitable to man."

"The members of this high council would be free from research and teaching. They would dedicate their lives to the contemplation of the economic, sociological, psychological, physiological and pathological phenomena manifested by the civilized nations and their constitutive individuals. They would endeavor to discover how modern civilization could mold itself to man without crushing any of his essential qualities. Their silent meditation would protect the inhabitants of the new city from the mechanical inventions which are dangerous for their body or mind, from the adulteration of thought as well as food, from the whims of the specialists in education, nutrition, morals, sociology, etc., from all progress inspired, not by the needs of the public, but by the greed or illusions of their inventors. An institution of this sort would acquire enough knowledge to prevent the organic and mental deterioration of civilized nations. Its members should be given a position as highly considered, as free from political intrigues and from cheap publicity, as that of justices of the Supreme Court. Their importance would in truth, be much greater than that of the jurists who watch over the Constitution. For they would be the defenders of the body and the soul of a great race in its tragic struggle against the blind sciences of matter."

This elaborate scheme seems in direct contrast to opinions he expressed early in the book: "Modern civilization absolutely needs specialists. Without them, science could not progress. But, before the result of their researches is applied to man, the scattered data of their analyses must be integrated in an intelligible synthesis."

"Such a synthesis cannot be obtained by a simple roundtable conference of the specialists. It requires the efforts of one man, not merely those of a group. A work of art has never been produced by a committee of artists, nor a great discovery made by a committee of scholars. The syntheses needed for the progress of our knowledge of man should be elaborated in a single brain."

Here Carrel displayed characteristics that he vigorously warned against: "Scientists who have strikingly distinguished themselves by great discoveries or useful inventions often come to believe that their knowledge of one subject extends to all others. Edison, for example, did not hesitate to impart to the public his views on philosophy and religion. And the public listened to his words with respect, imagining them to carry as much weight on these new subjects as on the former ones. Thus, great men, in speaking about things they do not thoroughly understand, hinder human progress in one of its fields, while having contributed to its advancement in another."

*Man, the Unknown* received high critical acclaim by many reviewers but not by all. One favorable contemporary review typifies the favorable comments: "The Preface shows clearly the humility of a great man. The book offers opportunity for a better understanding of human beings and of life, not only to the scholar but to every thoughtful person. It stands alone in its particular effort and accomplishment and is most interesting and valuable."

*Time* Magazine of September 16, 1935, was quite cryptic in its review: "In his mighty flight of fancy Dr. Carrel does not pause to explain to men of lesser minds just how, as a practical political matter, these titanic reforms are to be brought about. Nor does he adduce any historic arguments to prove that doctors make great governors of men, perhaps because such arguments are difficult to find. U.S. experience with doctors in high office (e.g. New York's Senator Royal S. Copeland and Representative William Irving Sirovich) Dr. Carrel apparently realized would not help his point."

"Dr. Carrel is a great medical scientist, an avid mystic who knows no intellectual bonds. He is, besides, a sly mocker who delights in wild rant. Whether his thesis of iatrocracy was meant to be a colossal joke with which to fool members of his profession or whether he offered it in all earnestness with the idea that it would add to his stature as a world thinker he alone knew last week."

The *British Medical Journal* published a review by Sir Arthur Keith, who noted Carrel's belief in clairvoyance, telepathy and the power of prayer to heal even when the patient does not participate in the prayer. Observing that "Dr. Carrel, the man of science, shelters under the same hat as Dr. Carrel the mystic," Keith added, "Those of us who believe that the art of healing can be advanced only by careful observation, clear-cut experiments and sound reasoning will have Dr. Carrel cast in our teeth by charlatans . . . who believe there is a shorter road. Medical men ought to be familiar with *Man, the Unknown*. In reality, it reveals more concerning Dr. Alexis Carrel than about Man."

In spite of these critical reviews, including several by the Catholic Church based on his support of eugenics, *Man the Unknown* found a large popular audience suggesting that men were indeed anxious about their future on this planet. Not only in France and America, but all over the world several successive editions were absorbed by an avid and thirsty public.

As a result, Carrel was asked to speak at a number of universities and organizations. He received the Cardinal Newman award and delivered an address covering the same material before the Newman Foundation at Champaign, Illinois.

In the late 30's and early 40's, a number of articles appeared in *The Reader's Digest* written by Carrel. They include "Breast Feeding of Babies," "Married Love," "Prayer is Power," and "Work in the Laboratory of Your Private Life." Each was beautifully written and clearly demonstrated Carrel's facility with the English language. It is also obvious that Carrel had carefully researched the best medical thinking of the time. Each article, however, emphasizes his strong feeling of the need of self-discipline, self denial, hard work, and thorough study as the way to achieve happiness. He cautions, "Unless we emulate certain worthwhile features of Fascist education—notably their discipline and utilization of every working hour—we shall be no match for the tougher products that result from such an education. Democracy may have to be defended on the battlefield. Can it be adequately defended by those who spent their adolescence listening to radio romances, or expressing their pitiful little personalities in water colors and tantrums."

"Prayer is Power," the last of this series appearing in March, 1941, took a different tack. He stated that even our slightest impulse toward prayer has a dynamic, beneficial effect upon our lives. "If you make a habit of sincere prayer, your life will be very noticeably and profoundly altered. Prayer stamps with its indelible mark our actions and demeanor. A tranquility of bearing, a facial and bodily repose, are observed in those whose inner lives are thus enriched. Within the depths of consciousness a flame kindles. And man sees himself. He discovers his selfishness, his silly pride, his fears, his greeds, his blunders. He develops a sense of moral obligation, intellectual humility. Thus begins a journey of the soul toward the realm of grace."

"How does prayer fortify us with so much dynamic power? To answer this question (admittedly outside the jurisdiction of science) I must point out that all prayers have one thing in common. The triumphant hosannas of a great oratorio, or the humble supplication of an Iroquois hunter begging for luck in the chase, demonstrate the same truth: that human beings seek to augment their finite energy by addressing the Infinite source of all energy. When we pray, we link ourselves with the inexhaustible motive power that spins the universe. We ask that a part of this power be apportioned to our needs. Even in asking, our human deficiencies are filled and arise strengthened and repaired."

Carrel's religious education as a child had not kept him active in the Catholic Church, yet he never denied his faith. He was critical over the years of Catholic dogma and of the temporal strength and materialism of the Church. In addition, he had at times been very critical of members of the clergy whom he had met in Canada and in France. Except for a few notable exceptions he had never been greatly impressed with the Catholic clergy he had met. He considered himself a free thinker, but certainly not an atheist. He had been deeply moved in his younger days by the miraculous cures he had witnessed at Lourdes, but he left until his later years the process of revising his feelings toward them. In the mid-1930's when Carrel entered his sixties, he began more and more to search for the meaning of life. Among his scholarly friends he found no interest in discussions of this subject, and even among *the Philosophers,* especially since the serious illness and death of his friend P. Clifford, there was little interest. He therefore turned to the priests among whom he hoped to find some enlightenment. He met Father Sertillanges, an extremely intelligent Dominican, but Carrel soon felt rebuffed and regarded the Dominicans as impudent as he had found all other intellectuals. He was sad to discover the same qualities in Jacques Maritain, the brilliant philosopher whom he had known long before in New York. He found that the directors of the magazine *Intellectual Life* had, in his opinion, no contact with reality. In Brittany he thought perhaps he would find help among the monks, but found them "majestical without their feet on the ground." Finally Carrel heard of a monk, Dom Alexis Presse, whose description fascinated him. Dom Alexis was a Trappist, profoundly imbued with the spirit of St. Bernard. His very reformative ideas resulted in his exile with two of his companions to a small abandoned Abby at Boquen in the wilds of Brittany, not too far from St. Gildas. Dom Alexis had a magnetic personality, an emaciated face with tender but lively eyes, a poor stringy beard through which could be seen the bones of his chin. His hands were slender and nervous, and his feet always in slippers. He combined a deeply spiritual temperment with a strong temper which asceticism had hardly disciplined, and was always burning with enthusiasm from some great idea.

Carrel and his wife visited Dom Alexis for the first time in August, 1937 at his abandoned Abby. Carrel was much impressed with the openness of the man and a warm relationship began. They found they had much in common, both had mystical inclinations, and were prone to strong opinions and enthusiasms. Dom Alexis and Carrel corresponded frequently and visited together when possible over the next few years.

In 1935 Carrel began to work toward the development of an

Institute of Man. This was to be a central institution to guide research and to synthesize it for the use of modern man, following the precepts outlined in *Man, the Unknown*. An organizational committee was established to select 100 Founding Members to prepare the statutes and by-laws. Supervision would be exercised by a Board of Trustees of seven members chosen from among men of daring and initiative, who had already proven their ability as original thinkers. An annual budget of $100,000 or a capital of $2,500,000 was decided upon as the target financing to begin the Institute. Analysis and synthesis of all existing knowledge on such things as the best human diets, working conditions, methods of protecting the environment were primary projects of the Institute. More controversial projects would be the careful scientific investigation of clairvoyance, mental telepathy and other supernatural phenomena. By 1938 fund raising had begun and the Lindberghs offered the use of a family home, High Fields, near Hopewell, in New Jersey, 50 miles from New York. Several detailed programs of research had been planned and the budgets determined. But two things interrupted the great plans; no men of the high quality Carrel had envisioned could be enticed to join the Institute, and the last few years of the 1930's were filled with general anxiety from the eruption of the Second World War, which distracted everyone concerned. The Institute of Man remained a dream for the time being.

Carrel found himself at the height of his popular fame between 1931 and 1939. In early 1931 he received a notable honor. In Washington D.C. he received from the hands of the German Ambassador to the United States the distinguished Nordhoff-Jung prize. This was the first time the prize had been presented to anyone in the United States, and to a Frenchman. The German commission indicated that the prize was awarded to Carrel for his improvements in methods of tissue culture and for his use of tissue cultures in elucidating certain fundamental questions relative to malignant tumors. In 1936 he traveled and lectured in Germany; New York University awarded him the honorary degree of Doctor of Sciences. In December, 1936 he was elected associate member of the Academy of Sciences and Fine Arts in Lyon. In 1939, the Belgium Society of Biology welcomed him.

The highest spheres of international science honored him everywhere.

Still his interests during this period were leaning more and
more toward the philosophical and away from the biological. In
the summer of 1938 at Saint Martin-en-Haut he began in the
silence and solitude to work on a new book. The book was to be
entitled *The Conduct of Life* and was not completed at the time
of his death but was published posthumously. He wrote to a
friend, "I spent almost all my time trying to write a new book but
it is much more difficult than the first one. Besides the strange
atmosphere of worry which is spreading all over France and that
one feels around us doesn't constitute an appropriate environment
for intellectual work."

In a letter to a Lyonnaise friend written during this period,
Carrel commented: "Life becomes more and more surprising and
mysterious the more one lives. I feel that scientific research has
hardly touched the surface of what we would like. . . . As for
me, I experience the need to begin a new career because biological research as we know it leads only to insignificant things in
comparison with what is necessary and what must be done. . . .
The greatest successes of the physiologists will not prevent our
world from collapsing."

Simon Flexner retired as Scientific Director of the Rockefeller
Institute in October, 1935, and his successor did not have any
particular attachment for Carrel. This, combined with a general
reduction in the budget caused by the financial depression caused
Carrel, the "spoiled child" of the Institute since 1906, to complain
bitterly against economies which he considered "disastrous." The
general direction of work in the laboratories of the Rockefeller
Institute seemed to be oriented in other directions, and the
portion of the total budget allocated to the Department of Experimental Surgery progressively decreased. For years there had
been antagonism and perhaps some jealousy toward the Nobel
Prize winner and the favored position he had held under Simon
Flexner. The hostilities he had sowed were showering down on
him. Carrel's political statements also, no matter how well meaning, such as his approval of the highly disciplined education
under the Fascists, were making him an even more controversial

figure around the Institute. He and Charles Lindbergh were strongly criticized for their approval of some of the features of national socialism, as Hitler's Germany was becoming ever more menacing and unpopular in the United States.

Carrel reached the age of sixty-five on June 28, 1939, the mandatory retirement age at the Rockefeller Institute. Even though he was no longer pleased with the atmosphere or the budgetary priorities, he did not want to give up his laboratory completely as he was told it would be necessary to do. At this time, without his knowledge, a friend, a very influential person, intervened in his behalf. In May 1939 she wrote in a letter to John D. Rockefeller: "I am sure you will acquit me of all suspicion of wanting to intervene in some way in the administrative affairs concerning the Rockefeller Institute reputed for a long time as the home of scientific research. I must write you this letter because I have the feeling that you don't realize that the departure of Dr. Carrel from the Institute because of the age limit will put an end to experiments which are considered and are, I am completely assured, of the most extreme importance. It has been insinuated that the termination of this work could be due to budgetary limitations. If this is really the case, I must advise you that there are friends of Carrel who have told me that they would undertake the collection of the necessary funds for the continuation of the research of Dr. Carrel at the Institute. Perhaps you are already familiar with this situation and you will give him consideration. Dr. Carrel doesn't know anything about my letter and if he were to learn about it, he would be very angry and would disapprove my writing to you."

A few days later Rockefeller responded that "The retirement because of the age limitation of people who have rendered valuable services in every branch whether it be science, education, etc., is always received with regret. The more valuable the service has been the greater is the regret when it ends. While formerly people continued to work as long as they were capable of working because no assurance had been taken for their old age, the tendency of our days is clearly in favor of such assurance and in favor of a formal retirement at a fixed age without regard to the occupation. It is not rare that this principle plays a disadvantage for the private enterprise of a qualified worker. When the principle was established at the Rockefeller Foundation and the General Education Board, I bitterly opposed it. It functioned for several years and although it had examples that were shown to be disadvantageous to organizations, I am becoming more and more convinced that this principle is wise. As for the retirement of the four eminent scholars at the Rockefeller Institute at the beginning of the summer, we can only say that in the case of each one that it would be wished that such a rule hadn't been applied. That is as it sits and I feel that from every point of view it is in the interest of the Institute. Happily for the men to whom I am referring, a provision exists which makes it possible to satisfy the demand of each one of them for laboratory facilities on a modest scale for an indefinite period after retirement. Such facilities are of course at the disposition of the four scholars. Although the facilities are generally of reduced proportion, the opportunity is nevertheless assured to each one of these men for the continuation of their research if they desire it. I presume in a general fashion that it is true in the domain of science and elsewhere that the greatest part of productive work in the world is made by people in the first part of their lives rather than in the course of their old age, although there are many remarkable exceptions. Thus, we are responsible for carrying on the work of the Institute and of dispersing the funds in the most sensible manner, and I am certain you are in agreement, though we may deplore the results in such an individual case. (Signed) J.D.R. P.S. It is interesting and pertinent to remember that the year after Mr. —— retired because of the old age limitation from the Board of Trustees of the Rockefeller Foundation, he was designated Chief Justice of the Supreme Court."

Thus after 33 years of service to the Rockefeller Institute, Carrel closed his laboratory June 30, 1939. In his bitterness at being forced to retire, in being treated like everyone else, he did not ask to retain a smaller laboratory. He denounced the Institute, and renounced scientific research. In July 1939, he and Madame Carrel sailed for France and for their retreat at Saint Gildas.

# CHAPTER IX

THE SECOND WORLD WAR

A FTER ARRIVING IN FRANCE, Carrel passed several relatively calm weeks on St. Gildas. He renewed many old friendships, and began to correspond frequently with Dom Alexis Presse. Alexis travelled to Boquen to study the trappists' ascetic life-style; Dom Alexis reciprocated by visiting his friend's island home. Carrel considered establishing permanent residence in France, but decided instead to return to New York. He notified friends that he would return in mid-September, but these plans were never to come to fruition.

On September 1, Hitler invaded Poland. Mobilization was immediately ordered throughout France. Carrel unhesitatingly decided to remain. He departed for Paris to obtain orders to the front. In Paris, he called on Minister of Health Rucart, and demanded that he be given either a laboratory position or be placed with the ambulance corps. Rucart responded, "That's very interesting. I have appointments every Wednesday; come talk to me then."

Carrel persisted; in October he was finally given an assignment. He was charged with "guiding the means of conservation and the transportation of blood over long distances." At that time, blood could be kept only a few days before it deteriorated completely. Normal plasma could be obtained only in limited quantities. Carrel considered manufacturing an artificial nutrient liquid similar to that used in the Lindbergh pump, but the details of the process were never completely ironed out. (A year later the problem was resolved in New York by the invention of dry plasma.) Carrel desperately desired to introduce in France the advanced means of administering oxygen in shock, pulmonary afflictions and high altitudes that had been recently developed in the United States. Above all, he wished to establish a laboratory of experimental surgery at the Pasteur Institute to facilitate the development of new surgical techniques.

In early January, 1940, Carrel obtained an audience with Dautry, one of the most influential ministers in the French government. Dautry had been favorably impressed by Carrel's former service to France. He granted Carrel a laboratory, and decreed that it should be built in one month's time. The architect Gessian (who was later to serve at Carrel's institute) was called in to draw up blueprints for its construction. Four weeks later, the one story brick building was completed. Personnel and laboratory equipment, however, were not forthcoming. The building remained, but was never put to any effective use.

James Wood Johnson, the director of the American Volunteer Ambulance Corps in France, visited the laboratory in April. He was interested in establishing a mobile hospital to serve the wounded at the front. He wanted Carrel to aid him in its design, but it would be necessary for them to go to the United States since only there could be obtained the necessary men and material. Carrel agreed. He booked immediate passage from Paris, but was unable to depart for several weeks, due to a slow-down in the trans-Atlantic communications network. He finally arrived May 28 in New York. The next day he met with Charles Butler, his architect colleague from the First World War, and with Johnson they began to design a one hundred bed hospital to serve the French army.

Three weeks later, all hopes for the hospital (in France) were suddenly shattered. On the evening of March 21, 1940, the Germans presented the conditions for an armistice to the French government. At ten o'clock the following morning, France accepted. That same day Marshall Petain presented the President of the Republic drafts of decrees naming Laval and Marquet as Ministers of State. President Lebrun at first refused his signature, but Petain persuaded him to sign. As far as France was concerned, the war was over. Ironically, the surrender took place at Compiegne, the very town where Carrel had served in the First World War. With France's defeat, the mobile hospital was offered to England and was used to great effect in the campaign for North Africa.

Carrel had foreseen the inevitability of France's defeat, but had never expected it so soon. As early as 1933, he had written

"An impending disaster looms over Europe." In 1937, he had denounced the Nazi regime as "rejecting classical culture, Christianity, the sacredness of human personality and liberty . . ." He characterized Hitler as a "prodigious phenomenon in the history of humanity—an uncanny and gigantic power, a conqueror more audacious than Tamerlane and Genghis Khan, a mystical teacher through whom the innermost soul of the people manifests itself, a clairvoyant who senses the future, who reaches his goal through cunning, crime and bloodshed with somnabulistic cruelty." Carrel maintained that "National Socialism has constructed a world that is not adapted to man as he is," and predicted that "this world will not last indefinitely." He asserted his contention that "at this moment the future of the civilized world depends upon the government of the United States." In addition, the United States must enter the war for its own protection since "even the immensity of the Ocean cannot protect America from its (Germany's) invasion."

Many Americans, including Colonel Charles Lindbergh, supported a policy of "America First" at this time; they believed there to be no clear and present danger to the territorial defense of the United States, and beseeched the United States government to avoid war. Carrel noted that "peace-loving people are signing petitions asking the government to keep this country out of war," but equated such isolationist sentiments to "(a shepherd's) power to protect his flock against the hurricane."

The signing of the Armistice disturbed Carrel immensely. He left immediately for the countryside where he remained in seclusion until the middle of September. On October 17, he received word that Madame Carrel was safe at St. Gildas. She had plenty of food but very little coal. The Germans had confiscated their two cars and their motorboat, but otherwise had been very courteous. She had refused to move and the Germans had made no attempt to force her to do so. However, they had occupied the Lindbergh's island, Illiec.

Greatly relieved, Carrel left for Washington to meet with his friend, J. W. Johnson, who was engaged in negotiations concerning the purchase of great quantities of vitamins from the United States government. Johnson planned to smuggle these vitamins into occupied France and to distribute them equitably among the many thousands of under-nourished children there. With Carrel's assistance, Washington was persuaded. The next day Carrel wrote: "My intervention was capital. I will be the cause of many children remaining alive who would (otherwise) have been dead in the era of destruction we are entering."

On February 1, Carrel and Johnson boarded a steamer bound for Lisbon. The voyage was extremely rough; the ship did not reach its destination until the 15th of February. Two days later Carrel wrote his secretary, "We are still in Lisbon, prevented from leaving for Madrid because of damages caused by a storm." The two finally arrived in Madrid on February 19.

They were appalled by the conditions they found. There was virtually no food to be had except for by the very rich. The average peasant had about one peseta (eight cents) a day to spend for food. Johnson noted, "Eggs cost one peseta each, butter is twenty pesetas a pound, sausage sixteen pesetas, fresh sardines three or four pesetas a pound. How can anyone eat on one peseta a day?"

Upon their arrival Carrel and Johnson were given a tour of the city. They passed a huge pile of bricks where several groups of people had gathered. "That tenement," their guide told them, "caved in last night. There are fourteen corpses, they say, in the cellar." As they continued, a group of small children approached the two foreigners. Johnson offered them some milk chocolate, which he had saved from Lisbon, since they appeared to be very hungry. Suddenly, hundreds of small children swarmed around them pleading that they be fed as well. "Come away quickly," urged their guide. "Soon there will be thousands here, from everywhere. Come away quickly, or you will be smothered."

The French doctor and his American friend returned to their hotel, The Ritz. The Ritz symbolized perfectly the vast gulf between prosperous upper class Spain and all of the others. Except for bread (which was replaced by small pieces of a concoction made from corn and beans), they could have anything they wished. For two dollars they were able to dine in elegance, when all around them people were starving.

The next day their guide led them to a children's dispensary.

The first case observed was a three year old boy who had a deep raw sore on his leg. Two months earlier he had scratched the leg on a splinter of wood. Instead of healing, the sore had formed. In another ward they found a three month old baby. Its mother had not been able to nurse it, and no condensed milk was available. Thus, the mother was feeding it the only liquid on hand—the water left from cooking carrots and a bit of boiled skim milk.

The data compiled confirmed that the mortality rate was gradually exceeding the rate of birth. The diet of the majority of the Spanish people was completely devoid of protein. No meat or its equivalent was available.

On February 26, Carrel and Johnson visited the Auxilio Social, the official government relief organization sponsored by the Falange (the Fascist part of General Franco which had recently come into power as a result of the Spanish Civil War). "Hot meals were being supplied to 100,000 persons a day in Madrid, about 25 percent of those in need. Of these meals, 25,000 were for children." The following morning they toured a large children's hospital. There they witnessed innumerable cases of atrophic infants—"mere skeletons, all eyes and ears, their poor little bodies shrivelled to not much more than just bones." Such children normally constituted 5 percent of all cases admitted into the hospital; they now constituted 60 percent.

As they were leaving the hospital, Carrel asked the head doctor if the subject of the revolution was still very much on his mind.

"Yes," answered the doctor, "you cannot understand what fear—terrible, constant, everlasting fear does to you. When every knock at the door might mean that your turn had come. The worst was when a car passed in the night. You heard the chug-chug-chug of a motor, and everybody in the building suddenly stopped talking. Stopped breathing almost. Then—ah, it has gone past."

"My brother," the doctor continued, "died for me. They shot him in my stead. So you see, we still live back in those days. I say to myself we must all think of pardon and try to work together, but I cannot do it. Not yet."

The two investigators drove to Toledo for the day on the

second of March. At Alcazar, they visited "a dungeon-like room" that had been converted from a chapel into a hospital. There "by the light of a lantern, wounds were dressed and limbs were sawed off with a meat saw, without anesthetic." Their queries determined that most of the deaths occurred as a result of pneumonia and heart disease. A local padre maintained that all records of death from heart disease were "just another way of saying that they broke down from starvation." The average daily diet consisted of a few acorns for breakfast, some orange peels at noon and maybe a dish of turnips or beets in the evenings. What a woman could hold in her hand was considered an adequate day's supply of food for four.

Carrel and Johnson returned to Madrid to be greeted by an editorial in the Franco controlled newspapers accusing Johnson of "under the guise of charity" being actively engaged in "Red propaganda." The article alleged that Johnson "distributed (in the company of a famous French doctor) money to the Reds, at the same time giving them political tracts." There was no foundation whatsoever for these charges. Carrel and Johnson had, in fact, given aid indiscriminately to both the supporters of the Franco regime and to their enemies, the so-called Reds, who had fought them in the Spanish Civil War. They had at no time possessed any papers that contained any mention of politics.

Dr. Carrel and Mr. Johnson left Spain for Vichy on March 15. They were unable to transport their cargo of vitamins into the occupied zone of France, so Johnson cabled the United States to ask what course of action should be taken. New York wired an authorization to distribute the vitamins in Spain; Johnson complied by making them a donation to the children's hospital in Madrid. Rumors abounded that Carrel and Johnson had committed double forfeiture by selling the vitamins to the Germans, but in fact, such rumors had no basis whatsoever.

At the Vichy airport, Carrel was swamped by journalists. His only comment to their intensive interrogation was, "I wasn't sent by anyone. I am not charged with any mission." The next morning Carrel met with Petain. The two conversed for several hours. They discussed at length what they perceived to be the intellectual and moral problems of France. They agreed that there must be a repression of alcoholism, an encouragement of family, a reform of public instruction. Carrel reported to Petain the results of his nutritional studies in Spain, and no doubt put forth the proposition of the formation of an Institute of Man to deal with all such problems.

On March 23, Carrel and Johnson departed Vichy for an automobile tour of the occupied zone. Carrel suffered an attack of acute conjunctivitis at Marseille on the 25th, but was able to travel again after a day of rest. They arrived in Lyon on March 28; Carrel visited his family, his former colleagues and passed a few peaceful hours at St. Martin-en-Haut. His impression of the effects of occupation upon the peoples of provincial France was anything but complimentary. He found there to be "an excess of wine, complete egoism. Nobody thinks of anything but food." The general population was making no effort to resist the Germans. "They assume the English will reestablish France in her former position."

At Aix en Provence, Carrel received a post card from Madame Carrel who was suffering at St. Gildas. He decided immediately to interrupt his inspection and rejoin his wife. He left the 4th by plane for Vichy. From Vichy he travelled by train to the coast, and boarded a petroleum boat for St. Gildas. He remained there until the 27th of May. Madame Carrel recuperated slowly; Carrel utilized his much cherished free time in deep spiritual discussion with Father Dom Alexis of Boquen.

Carrel was under great pressure at this time to return to the United States. He received letters and telegrams virtually every day urging his return, but decided that his famine studies must take first priority. The Germans authorities were extremely co-operative, and waived all visa requirements to facilitate his entrance into Belgium. Johnson asserted through the New York Times that Carrel was being detained by the Germans against his will, but no evidence was ever produced to corroborate this allegation.

Doctor Carrel proceeded through Belgium and returned to Vichy on the second of June. The Petain government offered him the chance to continue his studies; he accepted. They offered to subsidize his Institute of Man; again he accepted. Politics were of no consideration in the determination of this decision. The formation of the institute took precedence above all else. The government at Vichy was the de facto government of France. If he was to be effective in serving the people of France, he must work with them.

The whole of the summer and fall were consumed in the planning of the Institute. It was to be named the "Fondation Francaise pour l'Etude des Problems Humains." Many of the medical officers on Petain's staff resisted all efforts to establish the "Fondation." They questioned sarcastically the nature of "les problems humains" that it proposed to study, but their sarcasm was ignored. Carrel began to gather men of all professions from every part of France. These included philosophers, psychologists, psychiatrists, architects, political scientists, economists, and anthropologists as well as biologists and physiologists. The foundation was to be based upon Carrel's belief that all problems of man are interrelated. He believed that one man or one field of study is helpless to solve any human problem since its scope of knowledge is necessarily much too small. In Carrel's words: "Un homme seul ne peut rien faire." (One man alone can do nothing.) Thus, an institute must be established wherein men of all disciplines can come together to combine their knowledge for the common good. Carrel's recruits were almost exclusively young men (most of them were between 28 and 35 years of age) whom Carrel found to be more open minded than their senior counterparts.

The "Fondation Francaise pour l'Etude des Problems Humains" was sanctioned by law on November 17, 1941. Doctor Alexis Carrel was officially designated to fulfill the functions of its regent. The Vichy government made an original donation of 40 million francs (eight million dollars) for its funding. The foundation was charged with "researching all practical solutions and proceeding with all demonstrations in view of improving the physiological, mental and social conditions of the population."

Much of Carrel's foundation's early research centered upon the problems of children. Methods of controlling the number of children who are hereditarily well endowed and improving child development were studied respectively. The psychology of work was another early consideration. Methods of predicting illness, preventing fatigue and the prevention of early aging in workers were all thoroughly researched. The first definitive studies ever of the mental qualities of a population were undertaken.

Later in its existence, the foundation turned its eye to more controversial realms of study. Countless experiments were conducted in hypnosis, mental telepathy and extra-sensory perception. Madame Carrel was responsible, to a great extent, for this parapsychological emphasis. She had been fascinated by this field of study for years; indeed, many of her fellow researchers believed her to possess immense personal telepathic powers. Doctor and Madame Carrel often attempted direct communication by telepathy, and were reported to have been successful on several occasions.

Carrel and his wife suffered extensively during these war years. In their apartment the temperature was never above 43° Fahrenheit. The occupation authorities offered wood, but they refused it. Often, the food supply was insufficient. The Germans offered extra rations, but the Carrels refused to accept any more than the allotment for the general population. Madame Carrel lost 45 pounds. Despite his 70 years of age, Doctor Carrel was obliged to travel everywhere by bicycle. As a result, his health deteriorated greatly.

Fortunately, St. Gildas was never occupied. Carrel experienced there the only peace of his last five years of life. On the island, he devoted long hours to meditation, and wrote the bulk of *The Conduct of Life* which he had started years before. Within its pages, Carrel asserted his belief that "the lie has become the principle crime of the modern people." It is necessary to rid society of this practice since "it destroys community life and the life of nations. It is not enough, as Socrates taught, to merely understand virtue (in order) to become virtuous." Action must be taken to insure its implementation. Carrel stated further that "the freedom to conduct oneself of his own free will has never insured happiness," and implied that happiness can be obtained only if certain controls are placed upon man. Such sentiments are certainly not democratic, but are hardly an endorsement of the Third Reich (of which he was later to be accused). Indeed, this philosophy of behavior modification, although still controversial, has gained much acceptability in recent years, and has been practiced (in limited environments) with some degree of success in the United States.

Carrel associated with the Germans only when such association was absolutely necessary for his work. He did, on occasion, visit the German embassy, but "only to argue against the closing of the institute, which the Germans at one time were going to do, and to negotiate with them the problems of operating his institute . . ." On one occasion, the Carrels' were asked to come to the embassy on matters of business. When they arrived, they found a party in progress of which they had not been informed. They stayed "as short a time as they felt they could," and returned to their apartment. Some members of the French Resistance seized this opportunity to accuse Carrel of blatant collaboration, but these charges were never substantiated.

On March 2, 1942, Carrel wrote the German command from Paris that the foundation had "concluded an accord with the American hospitals through which the accidents of war will be treated after March 1 in this hospital." He stated his "natural desire that the wounded be treated with the best and most modern methods, particularly concerning anesthesia. The man who is most up to date with modern methods of anesthesia is Dr. M. B. Saunders (an American) who is being held prisoner at Compiegne." Carrel asked that Saunders be released. The Germans complied!

Carrel accepted subsidies and encouragement from the Petain government, but he shunned all political functions. He was offered the Presidency of the French Red Cross; he refused it. Minister of State Laval offered Carrel the directorship of the Public Health; he declined, feigning incompetence. In 1944, Laval offered Carrel the post of French ambassador to Switzerland. Carrel declined officially for reasons of failing health, but in actuality had no intention of leaving his work for any political position.

In the laboratories of the "Fondation Francaise pour l'Etude des Problems Humains," no mention of politics was permitted. Carrel took no part in activities not concerned with the foundation, but such neutrality could hardly be attributed to his younger colleagues. Many of them were in fact active members of the Resistance. These researchers reported to work many mornings unshaven and dirty from their activities of the preceding night. Carrel "looked directly into (their) eyes and demanded no explanation." On occasion he was said to wink knowingly as they entered the laboratories.

Despite the innocence of his behavior, rumors abounded that Carrel was indeed a collaborator. Those chapters of *Man, the Unknown* praising the superior organization of authoritarian regimes were quoted as evidence. The name Alexis Carrel was blacklisted in Algiers as well as in many parts of his native France. Leaders in the Resistance who had no contact with their compatriots at the foundation had Carrel placed under constant surveillance. Doctor Carrel's former student and friend Lecomte du Nouy echoed the charge of collaboration. His wife, who had been denied a position at the Rockefeller Institute, due (in her opinion) to the efforts of Madame Carrel quoted Madame Carrel as saying: "My dear Alexis has gone crazy. He has sold himself to the Germans." This statement was given much credence in influential Parisian circles, and inflicted great damage to Carrel's reputation.

In August, 1943, Carrel suffered a mild heart attack at St. Gildas. Due to an insufficient food supply and the complete lack of medical care, his condition worsened. His breath shortened, he suffered hepatic engorgement and swelling of the ankles. His condition became so serious that he was rushed by canoe to the coast and by automobile and finally night train to Paris. Several of his assistants met Carrel at the station, and immediately placed him in the hospital. Professor Donzelob examined him the next day and turned him over to his student Nouailles. A few weeks later, with proper medical attention, he had recovered sufficiently to resume his functions at the foundation. He seemed to have recovered completely; he climbed the six flights of stairs to work every day with relative ease. (The foundation's elevator was inoperative due to restrictions of electrical currency.) The work of the foundation continued as if nothing had happened.

Then, in August 1944, Carrel suffered a second, more serious, cardiac failure. As a result, he was reduced to a state of quasi immobility. Never again did he walk the streets of Paris. He was confined to his apartment and spent most of his days extended in an arm chair. He knew of the foundation's progress only through news brought by friends. The Americans had liberated France and a new left-wing government had come into power. Carrel was notorious for anti left-wing statements and had often maintained that if forced to choose between Fascism and Communism, he would take the former without hesitation.

One of the first orders issued by the Fourth Republic's new Minister of Health Valery Radot suspended Carrel from all responsibilities as regent of the institute. A "purging" committee was set up to determine the extent of Carrel's collaboration. Several leading figures in French medicine condemned anyone who would render medical aid to such a traitor. The media charged that Carrel was "a racist, a Nazi apologist and a Nazi eugenicist . . ." The police repeatedly invaded the privacy of his home to "insure that he had not fled the country." Charges that he had attempted "to supplant French universities with his foundation by forcing university laboratories to close when their staff members were reluctant to join his institute" were aired throughout Paris.

This turn of events produced a psychological shock in Carrel that rendered him "sad, sullen and depressed." His friend Frederick Coudert travelled to Washington to enlist Undersecretary of State Stimson's aid in clearing Carrel of all charges. Stimson telegraphed General Eisenhower and asked that he insure that Carrel not be arrested. Meanwhile, the French government continued to search for evidence with which to prosecute him. September and October of 1944 passed slowly; Carrel was neither arrested nor cleared. A few of the faithful visited on occasion, but there was little they could do to encourage Doctor Carrel. Towards the end of October, he suffered a complete physical collapse. By November 2, his condition had become so grave that Father Dom Alexis was notified at Boquen that his friend was at the brink of death. He departed Boquen immediately for Paris, and arrived November 4 after a 36-hour trip in a full train. Carrel had lost consciousness. Dom Alexis, Madame Carrel and the sisters of St. Vincents de Pau remained at his side throughout the night. At 2:00 P.M., November 5, 1944, the French radio reported that Dr. Alexis Carrel had fled his home to avoid standing trial for collaborationist activities. Carrel had been dead more than nine hours.

# EPILOGUE

At 7:00 that evening, the radio announced that it had been in error. They admitted: "Contrary to what we previously announced, Dr. Alexis Carrel died this morning of a cardiac crisis in his Parisian home," but the irony remained. He was buried in the Chapel of St. Yves near his house on St. Gildas. The Foundation was dissolved in 1945 and its duties assigned to the National Institute of Demographical Studies and Scientific Research. To this day, many reputable French physicians refuse to discuss Doctor Carrel because of the myth of collaboration that is still very much alive. However, no proof of such collaboration has ever come forth and at this late date, it is unlikely that any will.

# SOURCES

Alexis Carrel (June 28, 1973–November 4, 1944). *Twentieth Century Authors*, 1944.

Carrel's Man. *Time*, September 16, 1935, pp. 40–43.

Carrel, A.: Le goitre cancereux. *Thesis Medicine*, Lyon No. 147, Paris, Bailliere, *1*:303, pp. 1901.

————: Une querison a Lourdes, *Le Nouvelliste de Lyon*, 1902.

————: Anastomose bout a bout de la jugulaire et de la Carotide Primitive, *Lyon Med*, 99:114, 1902.

————: Presentation d'un chien porteur d'une Anastomose Arterio-Veineuse. *Lyon Med*, 99:152, 1902.

————: Les anastomoses vasulaires et leum technique operatoine. *Union Med Can*, 33:521, 1904.

————: La transplantation des veines et ses Applications Chinurgicales. *Presse Med*, 13:843, 1904.

————: The transplantation of organs: a preliminary communication. JAMA, 45:1645, 1905.

———— and Guthrie, C. C.: Functions of a transplanted kidney. *Science*, 22:473, 1905.

———— and Guthrie, C. C.: Extirpation and replantation of the thyroid gland with reversal of the circulation. *Science*, 22:535, 1905.

————: Surgery of blood vessels and its applications to the changes of circulation and transplantation of organs, *John's Hopkins Hospital Bull*, 17:236, 1906.

———— and Guthrie, C. C.: Complete amputation of the thigh with replantation. *Am J Med Sci*, 131:297, 1906.

———— and Guthrie, C. C.: Results of biterminal transplantation of veins *Am J Med Sci*, 132:415, 1906.

———— and Guthrie, C. C.: Uniterminal and biterminal venous transplantations. *Surg Gynecol Obstct*, 2:266, 1906.

———— and Guthrie, C. C.: Successful transplantation of both kidneys from a dog into a bitch with removal of both normal kidneys from the latter. *Science*, 23:591, 1906.

———— and Guthrie, C. C.: A new method of homoplastic transplantation of the ovary. *Science*, 23:203, 1906.

———— and Guthrie, C. C.: The reversal of circulation in a limb. *Ann Surg*, 43:203, 1906.

———— and Guthrie, C. C.: Anastomosis of blood vessels by the patching method and transplantation of the kidney. *JAMA*, 47:1648, 1906.

————: Heterotransplantation of Blood Vessels. *Science*, 25:740, 1910.

Carrel, A.: Experimental surgery of the aorta by the method of meltzer and aner. *JAMA, 54:28, 1910.*

————: On the experimental surgery of the thoracic aorta and heart. *Ann Surg, 52:83, 1910.*

————: Graft of the vena cava on the abdominal aorta. *Ann Surg, 52:462,* 1910.

————: Latent life of arteries. *J. Exp Med, 12:460, 1910.*

————: The treatment of wounds. *JAMA, 55:2148, 1910.*

————: Peritoneal patching of the aorta. *J Exp Med 12:139, 1910.*

————: Remote results of replantation of the kidney and the spleen. *J Exp Med, 12:146, 1910.*

———— and Burrows, M. T.: Cultivation of adult tissues and organs outside of the body *JAMA, 55:1554, 1910.*

———— and Burrows, M. T.: Cultivation of sarcoma outside the body—a second note. *JAMA, 55:1379, 1910.*

———— and Burrows, M. T.: Cultivation *in Vitro* of the thyroid gland. *J Exp M. 13:416, 1911.*

————: Permanent intubation cf the thoracic aorta. J Exp Med, *16:17,* 1912.

————: Experimental operations on the orifices of the heart. *Ann Surg, 60:1, 1914.*

————: On the technique of intrathoracic operations. *Surg Gynecol Obstet, 19:226, 1914.*

———— and Tuffier, T.: Patching and section of the pulmonary orifice of the heart. *J Exp Med, 20:3, 1914.*

———— and Dehelly, G.: *The Treatment of Infected Wounds.* New York, Hoeber, 1916.

————: Essential characteristics of a malignant cell. *JAMA, 84:1795,* 1925.

————: *Man The Unknown.* New York, Harper & Brothers, 1935.

———— and Lindbergh, C. A.: Culture of whole organs. Science, *31:621,* 1935.

———— and Lindbergh, C. A.: *The Culture of Organs.* New York, Hoebner, 1938.

————: Breastfeeding of babies. *Reader's Digest,* June 1939.

————: Married love. *Reader's Digest,* July 1939.

————: Work in the laboratory of your private life. *Readers Digest,* September 1940.

————: Prayer is power. *Reader's Digest,* September 1941.

————: A voyage to Lourdes. *Reader's Digest,* Book Section, September 1950.

————: *Reflexions Sur la Condnite de la Vie.* Paris, Libraine Plon, 1950.

Deterling, R. A., and Carrel, Alexis: The man and his contribution to vascular surgery. *J Cardiovasc Surg, 2:81, 1961.*

Corner, George W.: *A History of the Rockefeller Institute* (1901–1953). New York, The Rockefeller Institute Press, 1965.

Durkin, Joseph T.: *Hope for Our Times.* N.Y. Harper & Row, 1955.

————: *The Strange Pro-Nazism of Alexis Carrel.* In Press, 1973.

Conversation with Gessain (on tape) Carrel Collection, Georgetown University Medical Library.

Conversation with Gros, Merlet, Lombard, Ribollet, Crepin and Menetrier (on tape). Carrel Collection, Georgetown University Medical Library.

Johnson, James Wood: We saw Spain Starving. *Saturday Evening Post,* June 28, 1941.

Lindbergh, Chas. A.: *The Wartime Journals of Charles A. Lindbergh.* New York, Harcourt, Brace, Javanovich, 1970.

Lindbergh, Chas. A.: Preface de Colonel Charles A. Lindbergh. In Alexis Carrel. Savant, Mystique by Joseph T. Durkin. Fayard, Paris, 1969.

Smith, Robert B.: Alexis Carrel, 1873–1944. *Inves Urol,* 5:102, 1967.

Soupault, Robert: *Alexis Carrel, 1873–1944.* Paris, Libraine Plon, 1952. Visionary Scientist. *M.D.,* April 1973. pp. 129–134.

# INDEX